Visitor's Guide to the English Cotswolds

3rd Edition

By Blair Howard

This guide focuses on outdoor and recreational activities. As all such activities contain elements of risk, the publisher, author, affiliated individuals and companies disclaim responsibility for any injury, harm, or illness that may occur to anyone through, or by use of, the information in this book. Every effort was made to insure the accuracy of information in this book, but the publisher and author do not assume, and hereby disclaim, liability for any loss or damage caused by errors, omissions, misleading information or potential travel problems caused by this guide, even if such errors or omissions result from negligence, accident or any other cause information or for any potential travel problems caused by this guide.

Important Note: The rates for accommodations – hotels, inns, pubs, bed & breakfast, etc. - fees, prices, and especially the entrance fees to the many attractions, quoted throughout this book were current at the time of writing. However, they are all subject to change without notice and they do, **almost weekly**, thus the prices quoted herein are given only as a rough guide as to what you might expect to pay. The author therefore disclaims any liability for such changes and urges you to check, either by phone or online for current rates before you travel.

Table of Contents

This is the second edition of the Visitor's Guide to the English Cotswolds: more maps, photographs, places to visit, sights to see, places to stay- including bed and breakfasts - best pubs, and much more.

They say that a picture is worth 1,000 words. I hope that's true, because I have included more than 160 photographs in this book. The photos will, I think, help you to get a better idea of just how beautiful the English Cotswolds really are. Enjoy!

Map of the English Cotswolds

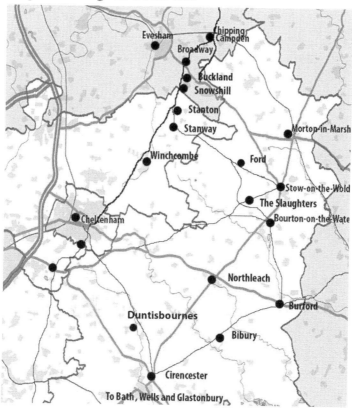

The English Cotswolds are a chain of undulating, limestone foothills that encompass a quiet, idyllic world of sleepy little towns and villages nestled among the hills and dales of central England. Rising to just over 1,000 feet at the highest point on Cleeve Hill, the Cotswolds are spread across a half-dozen west midland counties, including Gloucestershire, Avon, Wiltshire, Hereford and Worcester and Oxfordshire.

Bourton on the Water – Courtesy of Saffron Blaze and Creative Commons

For more than 90 miles, from Meon Hill just six miles south of Stratford-Upon-Avon, they stretch westward across the heart of England all the way to the great Roman City Bath. For more than a thousand years these pastoral, rolling hills have been home to more than a few of England's kings and queens, to its rich and famous, to farmers and shepherds and… well, to me.

To paraphrase, just a little, they do say you can take the man out of the hills, but you can't take the hills out of the man, and it's true. My earliest real memories of the Cotswolds date back to my childhood, the late 1940s. I remember the bus rides my mother and I took from Evesham to Broadway and then the seemingly long hike up the hill to Broadway Tower and the picnics we enjoyed looking out over the fabulous Vale of Evesham; balmy days indeed, were those.

But that was just the beginning. For more than 40 years, I lived, loved, got married, had two kids, five grand kids, hunted, got drunk, raised hell, played golf and fox hunted among the Cotswolds. The Cotswolds were my home and, even today, I visit as often as I can.

Cotswold Stone Cottages in Upper Slaughter - Courtesy of Trevor Rickard and Creative Commons

Little has changed over the past 50 years, or so; oh, the roads are a little busier, so are the pubs, hotels and restaurants, but there's an air of timelessness among these ancient hills, honey-colored towns, villages and cottages. This, then, was my world, a world quite different to that you'll find in the average guidebook to the Cotswolds.

I see the Cotswolds, even the well-known sites, through different eyes than do the tour guides that steer visitors from one well-worn site to the next, never deviating from the pre-set tour of what *they* think you should see. But there's more, so much more.

Thatched Cottage in the Cotswolds
Courtesy John Smith and Creative Commons

So, if you decide to visit the Cotswolds, you'll find you have several options: you can take the "grand" tour under the wing of one of the "official" tour guides and skim quickly from one overworked attraction to the next; you can walk the Cotswolds via the famed Cotswold Way, a great way to visit and see some of the sites, if you have the time, and if you are fit enough to hike up hill and down dale for more than 100 miles; or you can hire a car, and visit my world, off the beaten path.

So please, allow me to introduce you to my Cotswolds. Yes, we'll visit all the well-known and "not-to-be-missed spots" along the way, but I'll take you to places very few visitors to the Cotswolds get to go.

Chipping Campden, Broadway, Stanton, Stanway, Snowshill, Bourton-on-the-Water, Stow-on-the-Wold, Naunton, Northleach, Chedworth, The Slaughters, Buckland, Winchcombe, Burford, Cirencester and Bath are just some of the towns we'll visit

Broadway's main street - Courtesy of Trevor Rickard
and Creative Commons.

The historic sites and attractions we'll visit along the
way include: Bellas Knap (an ancient long barrow –
burial mound), the Rollright Stones (a prehistoric stone
circle you're not likely to find in any other guide book).

We'll also visit the lavender farm at Snowshill, the
visually stunning ruins of the Roman Villa at Chedworth,
Sudeley Castle (home of Queen Catherine Parr, last wife
of Henry VIII), the ruins of Hailes Abbey, Broadway
Tower, the Great Tithe Barn at Littleton, the Fleece Inn at
Bretforton (one of England's oldest pubs), the Roman
Baths at Bath, the tiny church at Wickhamford where you
can visit the tomb of one of George Washington's
relatives, and many more too numerous to mention here.

You'll find information about where to stay and where
to eat: pubs, inns, hotels and bed & breakfast houses. All
the information you need to successfully plan your visit to
the Cotswolds.

The Gardens at Sudeley Castle, Winchcombe -
Courtesy of Saffron Blaze and Creative Commons

The Cotswolds have been designated a national area of great natural beauty, and rightly so, for they truly are one of the loveliest spots on earth.

The Cotswolds are known to have been inhabited for more than 7,000 years. The entire area is rich in the remains of its early inhabitants, including pre-historic, Neolithic, Bronze Age, Iron Age and Roman settlements, long barrows, round barrows, henges, hill forts and Roman towns, villages, villas and estates.

The Long Barrow at Belas Knap – Courtesy Nigel Homer and Creative Commons

Today, the local industry is, of course, tourism. The funny thing is, though, you'll find almost as many English tourists among the Cotswolds as you will international visitors; the English are dedicated hikers and these hills were made for walking. But tourism in the Cotswolds is a relatively new industry; this was once the heart of England's vast wool trade. And that explains the word. "Cotswold."

A combination of two old-English words: Cottes are, or were, sheep pens; wolds, or woulds, is the ancient term for the word hills. Sheep, then, as well may you imagine, have been at the heart of the culture, heritage and even the architecture of the Cotswolds since time immemorial. In fact, no one knows exactly when the first sheep arrived in these hills, or from where. Some would have it that the first sheep were brought to England by the Phoenicians; more likely, though, it was the Romans who introduced them to the Cotswolds. The Romans successfully invaded Britain in AD 45 and they settled here, and they brought their livestock with them.

The Romans were a very civilized people, used to good living, even in the far reaches of the empire, and they needed quality wool for their clothing and quality meat for their tables. The Roman Longwool was a big, white hornless sheep with a heavy fleece, ideal for the harsh environs of Roman Britain, but it was the Cotswold Lion that brought fame and fortune to the area.

The Cotswold lion was/is an ancient breed of sheep, large, hardy and with heavy fleece, a true Longwool. From the early middle ages, the "Lion" brought great wealth and fortune to the Cotswolds. Most of fine churches you'll see on your travels were built upon Lion money, as were the ancient abbeys, such as Hailes and Tewksbury – the Tewksbury Abbey mill and workshops can still be seen in Stanton. Wool was the most important product for the Cotswolds.

The local wool merchants prospered beyond their wildest dreams. The great Cotswold manor houses, tithe barns, and several hundred fine churches, large and small, all owe their existence to the wool trade.

The Cotswold Lion - Courtesy Creative Commons

But times were not always so idyllic in the Cotswolds. During the English Civil War, 1642 to 1645 and from 1649 to 1649, the Cotswolds were of great strategic importance. The Royalists, loyal to King Charles were, for a time, headquartered at Oxford while the Parliamentarians – Roundheads- under the command of Oliver Cromwell held garrisons at Gloucester and Bristol.

The first battle of the Civil War was fought on October 23rd 1642 at Edgehill, on the northern edge of the Cotswolds. The battle began late in the late afternoon, and was a long and bloody affair with no positive result for either side; the next day King Charles moved on toward London; the Roundheads to Warwick.

Architectural casualties of the war and its aftermath included sites at Chipping Campden and Winchcombe.

The boom-time for the Cotswold wool trade lasted for slightly more than 200 years, from approximately 1340 to 1540 with the export of top-quality wool to Europe. But wool was important not just to the Cotswolds: the proceeds of its export to the continent were a major source of revenue for the English economy, hence the fabled "woolsack" under the Lord Chancellor's bench in the House of Lords.

Cotswold wool merchants lived and did their business in the many market towns you'll find scattered across these hills. They collected the fleeces from the local farmers. The merchants the sold the fleeces on to the Wool Staplers, intermediaries who held their authority from the Crown, and the Staplers sold it on to the woolen industry all across England and Europe.

The export of fleece wool from England to the continent declined with the introduction of the wool mills into the Stroud valley and the production of local cloth became a second important industry for the Cotswolds. Its decline began with the advent of the industrial revolution in England: most of the nation's wool industry moved north to Lancashire; mills constructed there were more productive due to their access to fast-flowing rivers.

The Cotswold Lion, however, remained. In fact, meat – in the form of mutton and lamb - became yet another source of wealth for the local farmers, right up until the end of World War II when the demand for it declined to almost nothing. The old Cotswold Lion is still around, though the numbers are quite small. Those that remain do so mainly through the good efforts of the Rare Breeds Survival Trust and the Cotswold Farm Park at Guiting Power, one of the Cotswolds' major tourist attractions.

And talking of major tourist attractions, during the last 50 years, or so, the Cotswolds have become one in their entirety. The tiny towns and villages, such as Broadway, Buckland, the Slaughters, Chipping Campden, Snowshill,

Stow-on-the-Wold, Stanton, Bourton of the Water, Guiting Power, Ampney Crucis offer a unique and relaxing holiday destination. And there are many, many more.

The Main Door to the Church of St. Edward in Stow on the Wold, guarded by two ancient yew trees – Courtesy of Martyn Gorman and Creative Commons

Just a few of the Cotswold villages and market towns have garnered international attention (they are the ones you'll find on the guided tours), but almost all of the rest of them are equally attractive; each has its own unique personality, and all are visually stunning. If you are planning your first visit to the Cotswolds, I envy you. You are in for a rare treat.

The Tiny Cotswold Village of Yanworth – Copyright
© Blair Howard

There are several ways to organize your visit. You can take a day out from your busy schedule in London and drive the 90 miles to spend a day visiting the half a dozen or so of the towns and villages that are located on or close to the A-429. Or you can do it right: rent a car and spend a week touring the highways, byways and back roads

You can live like a lord and stay in some of the finest hotels in the world, you can spend your nights in any one of a hundred inns or pubs, or you can live like a local in one of the many bed-and-breakfast establishments. Whatever you decide, you're in for a treat.

The Model Village at Bourton on the Water- Courtesy of Adrian Pingstone and Creative Commons

There are many beautiful villages in the Cotswolds, almost all of them less than 100 miles from London. Villages where you can sit in a shaded garden and enjoy a strawberries and cream tea, visit a country pub and enjoy a pint of local beer and a plowman's lunch beneath the heavy wooden beams.

You can stroll the streets of Bourton on the Water where the tiny river Windrush threads its way, like a jeweled ribbon, through the center of the town. You can visit Stanway, Lower Slaughter, Stanton, and Winchcome with its ruins of Sudley Castle, a drive of not much more than 15 miles in all.

St. Mary's Chapel and Gardens at Sudeley Castle, Winchcombe - Courtesy of Jason Ballard & Creative Commons

Each year many thousands of folks visit Great Britain, but most of them never get to see England as it really is. They make the rounds of the famous landmarks and the established tourist traps -- Anne Hathaway's cottage, Windsor Castle, The Tower of London, Stonehenge, and so on. Unfortunately, though, they miss the sweet side of

14

England. So a visit to the Cotswolds is a visit everyone should try to make, at least once.

This book is ordered somewhat geographically from east to west, and designed more to suit driving than walking, although there will plenty of opportunities along the way to take a stroll, even a longish walk, should you so desire.

There are several population centers, none of them large, where you can establish a base, with accommodations, or you can simply hop from one small town or village to the next, staying the night at one of the many hotels, inns, or bed-and-breakfast offerings along the way. I'll list some ideas for you to consider.

St. Barnabus Church in Snowshill – Courtesy Trevor Rickard and Creative Commons

We start out in the east at Chipping Campden and end basically in Bath (or you could do it the other way round), with many a side show in between, including some that are never included in guide books to the Cotswolds: Evesham, for instance – just five miles from Broadway, but a rare treat and well worth a visit. The Rollrights where you'll visit their version of Stonehenge – smaller, but just as fascinating. Snowshill is not on any tour I know of, but it should be. Chedworth is home to an amazing Roman villa, what remains of it, that is, a must see, in my opinion.

Note: Throughout this book, you'll find I've used the words "honey-colored" to describe the villages, and the stone from which they were built. I did this out of respect for the local convention. My own preference would be "golden," for no other word can adequately describe the sight of those beautiful Cotswold stone structures basking under the springtime, summer or even winter sunshine; it's an absolutely glorious sight.

Accommodations

When I travel the Cotswolds I rarely bother to book accommodations in advance. I prefer instead to take a pot-luck approach and get what I can where I can. There's nothing quite like visiting one of those little out-of-the-way villages and spending the night in an old-world pub or farmhouse or B&B (bed and breakfast) with full English (heart attack) breakfast included in the almost always very reasonable price of the room.

Less adventurous types might think this approach is a bit hit-and-miss, and that there's always the chance of not finding a room. Not so. At least it's never happened to me; there are far too many rooms within 10 miles of any given spot in the Cotswolds for this to happen. I know, my family used to run a B&B.

Many private homes offer bed and breakfast as a way of making a little extra cash; these are often the best value for money: you live with the family and you eat what they eat. Just look out for small signs in the front windows, pick your fancy, knock of the door or ring the bell, and ask the question.

Buckland Manor – Luxury Hotel – Copyright © Blair Howard

As I've already mentioned, accommodations in the Cotswolds vary across the board, from the local Bed & Breakfast (B&B) to the "Luxury" hotel, with all sorts of odd opportunities in between, pubs and inns being the most popular among international tourists. Rates also vary across the board. You can expect to pay between £75 per night ($125) to as much as £350 ($550). You'll find I have recommended something to suit every budget. You'll find listings of accommodations, with rates at the time of writing, at the end of each section.

A Typical B&B in the Cotswolds – Copyright © Blair Howard

Important Note about Rates:

The rates for accommodations – hotels, inns, pubs, bed & breakfast, etc. - fees, prices, and especially the entrance fees to the many attractions, quoted throughout this book were current at the time of writing. However, they are all subject to change without notice and they do, **almost weekly**, thus the prices quoted herein are given only as a rough guide to what you might expect to pay. Please be sure to check, either by phone or online for current rates before you travel.

Me? I think the good old village pub is a great place to spend the night; most of them offer bed and breakfast, like the Eight Bells in Chipping Campden (see the photo), and are usually conveniently placed within the village or town community.

The Eight Bells Pub in Chipping Campden – Courtesy
Stephen McKay and Creative Commons

Chipping Campden, is the epitome of the small, Cotswold market town. Set within the Cotswold district of Gloucestershire, Chipping Campden can trace its roots all the way back to the 7th century and there's no doubt that the area was inhabited even before that during Neolithic times. In the 11th century, after the Norman conquest of England, it was recorded in King William's Domesday Book that the village had a population of 300.

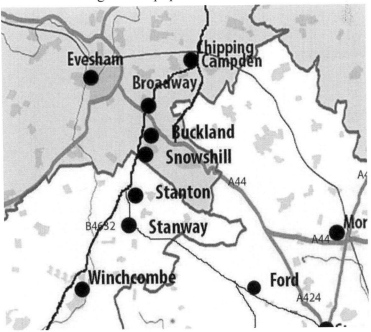

Map the Eastern Cotswold Villages and Towns

In 1185, King Henry II granted a market charter to the then Lord of the manor, Hugh de Gondeville, and thus Campden became Chipping Campden, chipping being the old English word for market.

The original layout of Chipping Campden's elegant terraced High Street was designed by de Gondeville, but most of the architecture you see today dates from the 14th century to the 17th century.

In 1380, William Grevel, a local sheep merchant, and one of the richest men in England, built for himself a house on the High Street. That house, Grevel House, still stands today. The Woolstapler's Hall was built a little later by Robert Calf, another big wheel in the local wool industry.

You'll absolutely love this quaint little town. I spent many an evening frequenting one pub or the other, and many's the Saturday afternoon I rummaged through the books at the Campden Bookstore. If you're to start your visit to the Cotswolds anywhere, I suggest you begin here in Chipping Campden.

What to See

To walk the High Street is a singular delight. An avenue of honey-colored limestone buildings, built from the mellow locally quarried oolitic limestone known as Cotswold stone, and boasts a wealth of fine vernacular architecture. At its center stands the Market Hall with its splendid arches, built in 1627.

The Market Hall – Courtesy Creative Commons

Chipping Campden was a rich wool trading center during the Middle Ages, and enjoyed the patronage of many a wealthy wool merchant.

Today, Chipping Campden is a popular Cotswold tourist destination, and the starting point for the Cotswold Trail, a walking trail that stretches for 102 miles all the way to City of Bath. At times, especially on weekends, it can be very busy; the pubs, tea rooms, restaurants and shops especially so, but Chipping Campden is an attraction not to be missed.

Be sure to take in the grand, early perpendicular wool church of St James – with its medieval altar frontals that date to the 14th century, its cope – 13th century - and its extravagant 17th century monuments to local wealthy silk merchant Sir Baptist Hicks and his family

Above you see the Church of St. James and the ruins of Campden House which was destroyed by fire during the English Civil War possibly to prevent it falling into the hands of the Parliamentarians. All that remains of this once magnificent estate are two gatehouses, two Jacobean banqueting houses, restored by the Landmark Trust, and Lady Juliana's gateway. The church and gatehouse together form a beautiful backdrop. – Photo credit: Colin Craig and Creative Commons.

Banqueting House & St. James' Church – Courtesy W. Lloyd MacKenzie and Creative Commons

St. James' Church – Courtesy Stephen McKay and Creative Commons

Take a quick peek at the Almshouses and Woolstaplers Hall. The gates to Campden House and the one-time wagon wheel wash, The Court Barn near the church is now a museum celebrating the rich Arts and Crafts tradition of the area.

The Alms Houses - Courtesy David Stowel and Creative Commons

The Gates to Campden House; the old wagon wheel wash is the depressed area at the right of the photo - Courtesy David Stowel and Creative Commons

The Campden Bookshop in Dragon House on the High Street has been a fascinating attraction for as long as I can remember. The shop offers a wide selection of guide books, books on the local Arts & Crafts Movement, art, and so on; it's also a fun place to just browse.

Mill Dene Gardens in Blockley are just a short four-mile drive (10 minutes) from Chipping Campden. This incredibly beautiful English water mill garden is situated on two-and-a-half acres of stunning Cotswold countryside. "Designed and planted in English country style," Mill Dene is a quiet world of beautifully landscaped terraces, water gardens, and scenic walks and pathways, all of which provide a delightful and relaxing couple of hours; this truly is Cotswold country at its best.

Mill Dene Garden Bells – Courtesy Graham Taylor
and Creative Commons

Hours:

Open three days per week Wednesday through Friday: 10 – 5pm (last entry 4pm); Saturdays: 9 - 1pm; Bank Holiday Sundays and Mondays, 2-5pm

Admission

Adults £7; Children under 15 £3; A short 10/15 min talk by the owner is available for individuals for £10, but you'll need to call ahead. Group rates - 20 people or more - £6.50 per person.

Contact: Mill Dene Garden, School Lane, Blockley, Moreton in Marsh, Gloucestershire, GL56 9HU; Phone 1386 700457; Email: info@milldenegarden.co.uk

Best Pubs:

No visit to Chipping Campden would be complete without a cool pint of beer and pub lunch. That being so, you might like to sample the fare at the delightful little Eight Bells pub on Church Street or the Kings Arms on High Street.

The Eight Bells – Courtesy Stephen McKay and Creative Commons

There are two famous and historic gardens nearby: at Hidcote Manor Garden, owned and managed by the National Trust, and at Kiftsgate, in private ownership but open to the public. Two miles to the west, in the grounds of Weston Park near Saintbury, are the earthwork remains of a motte and bailey castle.

The Ebrington Arms

The Ebrington Arms, just outside of Chipping Campden in the little village of Ebrington, is one of my old haunts from times gone by. It never changes; it remains one of just a few truly traditional Cotswold pubs.

A visit to this 17th Century inn is a memory in the making. Old-world English pubs like the Ebrington Arms are, today, as rare as hen's teeth, and this one retains many of its original, old-world features, including the inglenook fireplace, beamed ceilings and flagstone floors. But more than that, as steeped in history as it is, the atmosphere is palpable: you can almost cut it with a knife.

Photo Courtesy of Creative Commons and Kenneth Allen

Ebrington is an out-of-way, English Cotswold village where winding country lanes are punctuated by ancient thatched cottages. Ebrington is beautiful no matter when you visit, whatever the season and, close as it is to Chipping Campden, it could be the perfect place to begin your visit to the Cotswolds.

Where to Eat

The Ebrington Arms:

As I have mentioned already, the Ebrington Arms is an old haunt of mine. What I didn't mention is that the the pub specializes in fine dining. Known locally for the quality of its beer (very important) and for its excellent cuisine, old-world atmosphere and friendly owners – Claire and Jim Alexander – the Ebrington Arms is top of my list of places to eat, and it's a 4-star Visit Britain establishment too. Be sure to make a reservation. 01386-593223.

The Eight Bells:

The Eight Bells, on Church Street, pictured above, is a 14th century traditional Cotswold Inn featuring a nice menu of good food offered daily for lunch and dinner. Reservations: 01386-840371

Huxley's Café and Wine Bar:

A "period Café and wine bar" on Chipping Campden's High Street is just the place for a nice lunch or an afternoon tea with fancy cakes and a cup of tea or coffee. 01386-849077

Where to Stay

The Malins Bed & Breakfast Guest House

The Malins is actually in another little Cotswold village, Blockley, but is close enough to Chipping Campden. Jane Ricketts is the lady of the house and she offers a friendly welcome to her delightful Cotswold stone house." All rooms are en-suite (has a private bathroom) with TV, Tea/Coffee makers, radio alarms, hairdryer, magazines, and they come with a full English or continental breakfast. Malin's is a nonsmoking facility. The Malins, 21 Station Road, Blockley, Morton-In-Marsh. Tel: 01386 700402.

The Eight Bells

Pictured above, the Eight Bells on Church Street is a recently refurbished 14th century traditional Cotswold Inn offering fully en-suite B&B. The house offers fine dining with food available daily, midday and evening. Beautiful terraced garden. All rooms have TV and tea making facilities. Recommended by the 2003 Good Pub Guide. The Eight Bells, Church Street, Chipping Campden, Tel: 01386 840371

Folly Farm B&B

This lovely Cotswold cottage was once "a stable belonging to a village farm which has sadly long gone."

Today, the old stable has been fully restored, extended, and remodled to create the quintessential Cotswold bed and breakfast inn.

Facilities include three luxury guest suites, each with a private bathroom and either a four-poster or double bed.

Each room is individually styled with antique furniture, comfortable arm chairs, a flat screen TV and a DVD player and tea and coffee making facilities.

Folly Farm is non-smoking, and is unsuitable for children, and does not take pets.

The single occupancy rate is £55 per night, including breakfast; Double occupancy is from £36 per person per night.

Folly Farm is a 4-Star Visit Britain establishment.

Contact: Folly Farm Cottage, Back street, Ilmington, Warwickshire. CV36 4LJ; Phone 01608 682425; bruceandpam@follyfarm.co.uk

Gowers Close B&B

Gowers Close is a picture-book thatched cottage set in the charming village of Sibford Gower in the North Cotswolds with large windows that provide stunning views of the cottage gardens.

Not a large B&B: just two lovely guestrooms - one king sized double and one twin - both with private bathrooms, garden views, and tea and coffee making facilities.

So, if you're looking for somewhere special to stay, a relaxing weekend, long country walks, and hospitality you'll talk about for years to come, Gowers Close is exactly what you're looking for.

Gowers Close is in Sibford Gower some 14 miles from Chipping Campden, about 3/4 mile south of the B4035 between Banbury and Chipping Campden, and about 7 miles west of M40 (Exit 11).

Double occupancy is from £70.00 per night. Single occupancy £50.00.

Contact: Judith Hitching and John Marshall GOWERS CLOSE, Sibford Gower, Oxfordshire. OX15 5RW; Phone 01295 780348; Email: judith@gowersclose.co.uk

Here's an attraction you'll not find in many guide books. I used to visit the Rollrights when I was a child and, when they were old enough, I took my kids too. It's well worth a visit, and it's fun. Not only that, if you're driving in from London, to Chipping Campden or Broadway, you have to pass by the site, so it just makes sense to stop off along the way.

The King's Men - Copyright © Blair Howard

The Rollright Stones are part of a Neolithic site with origins lost in the mists of time. The old legends claim that the stones once were an ancient king and his knights turned to stone by a witch. The site has three main elements: the Kings Men stone circle, the King Stone, and the Whispering Knights.

The Rollright Stones are, in fact, a henge. Though not as spectacular as the more famous Stonehenge, a henge is what it is. The main circle, the King's Men, measures about 100 feet in diameter and set on top of a small ridge just off the main road.

The King's Men - Copyright © Blair Howard

Now, you can believe it or not, but there's a certain air of ancient mystery about this site. I remember when I used to visit that it was a very quiet spot, lacking even the sounds of the countryside – birds singing, the chirping and buzzing of insects, and so on. Well... maybe, maybe not; you'll have to judge for yourself.

One local legend has it that it's impossible to accurately count the number of stones in the circle. Maybe that's because of the numerous small stones, many of them partially hidden by the long grass and thus easily missed. Try it, it's fun, and I bet you come up with a half dozen different counts.

Just across the road from the Kings Men is the King Stone, a solitary monolith much bigger than those in the main circle. A few hundred yards further on along the path, you'll find another small group of stones, the Whispering Knights. This site once was "a turf-clad burial chamber."

The King Stone – Courtesy of Creative Commons

The Whispering Knights – Courtesy of Brian Robert
Marshall & Creative Commons

I really do recommend you take a few moments and visit. It's interesting, fun and a great photo op.

The Rollright Stones are located right on the Oxfordshire/ Warwickshire border just off the A44 close to Long Compton. From Chipping Campden, take the A44 through Morton in the Marsh. Traveling from London to Chipping Campden you'll be on the A44; watch for the signs. There's a small admission charge £1 (50p for children) which goes towards maintenance.

Hook Norton

Hook Norton is a small village, typical of the Cotswold brand, some five miles from Chipping Norton whose main claim to fame, other than its quaint little houses, shops and pubs, is its brewery. It a very old little community with its roots set deep in the dark ages.

Hook Norton Knights – Courtesy of David Luther Thomas & Creative Commons

There are stories of Viking raiding parties laying waste to what back then could only have been a small gathering of cottages. The Domesday Book, that great tome that records all that once belonged to William the Conqueror, states that in 1086 Hook Norton had population of 76 villagers and two mills, presumably flour mills.

Today, so they say, the village is known to its locals as "Hooky" and sometimes as "The Hook." Although not generally regarded as part of the Cotswolds, I have included it in this book for a couple of reasons: one, several readers have suggested that I do so; second, if you've decided to visit the Rollrights, Hook Norton is just a five minute, or so, drive away. It's a great place to grab a bite to eat and, of course, to visit the old Hook Norton Brewery. And, speaking of the brewery, I've done the tour myself and I highly recommend you do too; Everything about it is unique: the building itself, the interior, the working machinery, and the brewing **process; you get to see it all.**

How to Get There: Hook Norton is approximately five miles from Chipping Norton. From the A44, take the Banbury Road and drive five miles.

Hook Norton Brewery:

The brewery, founded in 1849, is a traditional Victorian tower brewing plant, thus its rather strange configuration. Strange looking it might be, but back in Victorian times, and even today, it incorporated the most efficient form of brewing processes: each stage in the brewing process flows downward from floor to floor; gravity being the most efficient method of transportation - mashing is don on the top floor, boiling in the middle, fermentation and racking at the bottom. Until 2006, the entire brewing process was powered by a Buxton & Thornley steam engine that has powered most of the machinery in the brewery since 1899. Quote: "It is the last commercially working open crank stationary steam engine in the UK. It is a small, simple engine consisting of a cylinder, flywheel, connecting rods and little else. The engine drives a system of shafts and belts connected to most of the machinery in the brewery; different sections of machinery can be engaged and disengaged by levers which slide drive belts on and off their wheels. Where there are gears in the line shafting, each pair consists of one iron and one wooden wheel. Thus, if any machinery should jam, only a few wooden teeth will be damaged and can then be replaced by the brewery's mechanics instead of needing a complex iron casting."

End quote. Today, the steam engine still runs but is used only to run the mashing equipment, the mill and the sack hoist. Beer is still delivered in the village the traditional way, by a horse-drawn dray (cart).

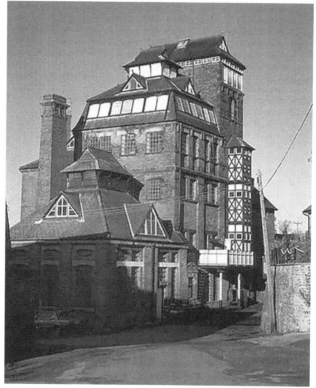

Hook Norton Brewery – Courtesy of Chis Allen & Creative Commons

Brewery tours every day, Monday through Friday at 11am and 2pm, and on Saturday at 11am and 1:30p. No tours on Sundays. To take the tour, you MUST book in advance by calling 01608 730384 or email: vc@hooky.co.uk

The tours last approximately 2 hours. You'll see the original steam engine, learn about the brewery's history and how the beer is made. If you visit of the right day, you can also see the beer being delivered to the local pubs, of which there are three. The great Shire horses can be seen Every Thursday (weather permitting), delivering to The Pear Tree at 12 noon; Every Friday, delivering to The Gate Hangs High at 12 noon. On the first Saturday of each month (again, weather permitting), the horses will leave the Brewery at 11am on a tour of Hook Norton. Contact: Phone: 01608 730384 or email: vc@hooky.co.uk

Cost: £12.50 per person (over 60 £10.00 per person). Allow two hours for your visit.

Best Pubs:

Hook Norton has four public houses. Three of them belong to the Hook Norton Brewery: The Gate Hangs High, the Pear Tree Inn, and the Sun Inn; all three serve beer produced by the brewery, and fine ale it is too. The forth pub in the village is the Bell.

If you decide to make a day-trip from London, and many people do, take the A-40 to Oxford, then the A-34 to Chipping Norton and then turn left onto the A-44 and drive on for about 16 miles and you will arrive in the tiny Cotswold village of Broadway.

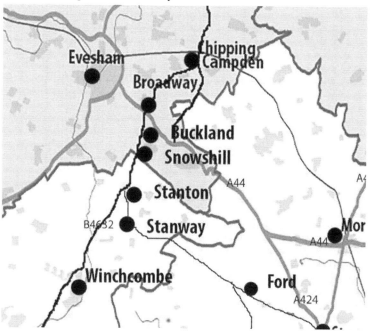

Map the Eastern Cotswold Villages and Towns

In the photo on the next page you see Broadway's main street looking from north to south: The Swan Inn is at the left of picture as you look at it; the village green is behind the lamppost at left and you can just see the Broadway Hotel at the extreme right. This photo was taken in the mid-1960s, but it could have been taken yesterday; little has changed. Photo courtesy of Creative Commons.

The photo below is a view of Broadway's main street -
Courtesy of Trevor Rickard and Creative Commons.

Broadway claims to be the most beautiful village in
England and, looking at the image above, who could
argue?

Broadway is, perhaps, the quintessential Cotswold
village. The natural stone cottages, and elegant homes,
house many of England's rich and famous. The cottages
were built mostly in the early 17th century and are
maintained today just as they were 300 years ago. The
Broad Way, or main street, features many antique shops,

art galleries, craft shops, pubs and tea rooms… and it's sad to say that Broadway, over the past 50 years or so, may have become the quintessential Cotswold tourist trap. Prices for all things, large and small, are higher in Broadway than almost anywhere else in the region. Be that as it may, Broadway is a delight and a must visit, just be careful and make sure you're getting value for money.

What to See:

Broadway Tower

Copyright © Blair Howard

Well, no visit to Broadway would be complete without a visit to the Tower. The top of the Tower is the highest point in the Cotswolds, and the view from the top is the best of more than 100 such views. Even from the foot of the Tower, the view over the Vale of Evesham is stunning; from the top, it's unbelievable.

The Tower was designed by James Wyatt in 1798 for the sixth Earl of Coventry, who probably had more money than sense. The Tower is built in the Norman style with three turrets and is surrounded by parkland. You can drive up the hill from Broadway, or you can hike it via a short section of the Cotswold Way: through the fields and kissing gates and over the wooden styles to the top, and then down again; it's a round-trip walk of about 5 ½ miles; allow at least three hours.

The Shops on the Broadway (actually called the High Street)

It's claimed that Broadway "has one of the longest village High Streets in the UK." I don't know if that's true, but it is quite a hike from the north end at the Swan Inn to the south end at the foot of Fish Hill. The lower high street is where you'll find all the shops, restaurants and tea shops; the upper high street offers photo ops of this quintessential Cotswold village: tiny, honey-colored cottages, some with thatched roofs, and grand old houses, all vying with one another to grow the best flower gardens, and grow them they do.

Church of St Eadburgha

The original parish church of Broadway, the Church of St Eadburgha has been a Christian place of worship since the 12th century.

Church of St. Eadburgha – Courtesy of Creative Commons

The current church was built circa 1400 but there are elements that remain of the original 12th century building.

The dedication of a Christian church to Eadburgha is not common. Eadburgha was the grand-daughter of Alfred the Great. As a child Eadburgha was asked to choose between receiving jewels or her own Bible, she chose the Bible. The church is listed as an English Heritage Grade I English Heritage Building.

There are at least a half-dozen fine country inns in Broadway. The most famous of these is the Lygon (pronounced Liggon) Arms. The inn was used at different times both by King Charles the first and by Oliver Cromwell. It was at the Lygon Arms that Edward the Eighth would secretly meet with Mrs. Simpson before he gave up the throne of England.

Recommended hotels are:

The **Lygon Arms**, Broadway. Worcestershire, WR12 7DU; Telephone: 01386-852255; Fax: 01368-858611. The Lygon is pricy, but you get what you pay for: a period room, many with wood beams, an extra comfortable bed and a full English breakfast (VAT included). Expect to pay in excess of £200 ($300) per night for a double room, but check the online booking sites and you'll probably find a good deal.

The Broadway Hotel, on the High Street, on the west side of the Village Green, a beautiful, old-world building in a captivating setting, and is just the spot to use as a base for your visit to the Cotswolds. The rates are reasonable, the food is good, and the beer is as good as it gets. For Bed and Breakfast, expect to pay, per night, from £80 ($130) midweek. to £160 on weekends, depending upon the size of the room. Broadway Hotel, The Green, Broadway, Worcestershire, WR12 7AA Phone: 01386 852401; Fax: 01386 853879. Email: info@broadwayhotel.info.

Russell's

This one I have little personal knowledge of other than the glowing reports I have received from relatives and friends living in the area.

An award-winning Cotswolds hotel and restaurant, Russell's is located in the one-time showroom of Sir Gordon Russell's furniture.

Russell's opened in 2004, following a massive restoration and conversion project that transformed a somewhat mundane, but historic building into what is today an elegant and locally famous 'restaurant with guest rooms available for visitors.

Russell's main claim to fame is its "modern, airy restaurant with terrace and private dining room."

The upper floor features "seven individually designed guest rooms and suites "all set in laid-back, stylish surroundings," including a suite, double and twin rooms – all with en-suite bathrooms, luxury bed-linens and air conditioning. Expect to pay: Double and Twin Rooms - from £105.00; Single Occupancy - from £90.00; Suite - from £235.00

All rates are quoted per room, per night and include accommodation, full English breakfast and VAT at 20%. Complimentary broadband access is available in all bedrooms. Russell's, 20 High Street, Broadway, Worcestershire,WR12 7DT; Phone 01386 853555; email info@russellsofbroadway.co.uk

Broadway B&B

Cowley House

Cowley House is right in the center of all that is Broadway. This one-time farmhouse and granary, now turned B&B, offers a unique bed and breakfast experience in a quiet location close to the village green. The owners, Joan and Peter Reading, are friendly and do their best to provide the best in hospitality and service.

The house, a beautiful Cotswold stone structure built in the mid-1700s, and its gardens provide an ideal opportunity to enjoy Broadway and the stunning Cotswold scenery. There are eight double/twin bedrooms, all with private or en-suite bathrooms. A hospitality tray, personal toiletries, hair dryer, TV, radio, alarm, fluffy bathrobes and magazines are available in each room. "Breakfast made with fresh, local ingredients." Joan and Peter will happily accommodate any special dietary requirements on request.

The Cowley House – Courtesy of Creative Commons

Cowley House is a non-smoking establishment. Children are welcome and so are well behaved dogs by prior arrangement. Parking is available.

Verdict: Cowley House is well situated close to the high street and local walking trails, which is a big plus. The owners are friendly, helpful and go out of their way to make your B&B experience a memorable one: breakfast is an experience all its own. Highly recommended.

Rates: Expect to pay between £78 and £99 ($125 and $160) per night; that well behaved small dog is £8 per night.

Contact: Cowley House, Church Street, Broadway, Worcestershire, WR12 7AE; Phone 01386 858148; Email joan.peter@cowleyhouse-broadway.co.uk; www.cowleyhouse-broadway.co.uk/

Mount Pleasant Farm

Maybe you'd like to try the English farm experience. If so, you might like to consider Mount Pleasant Farm, an 800 acre family farm just three miles from Broadway. The farmhouse breakfast includes home made jams and preserves and is served in the dining room; guests also have use of the lounge.

Mount Pleasant Farm

The farmhouse is located in the tiny village of Childswickham, just a short five minute drive from Broadway and Evesham. The setting is rural and the views are stunning. All the guest rooms have en-suite facilities, television, tea, and central heating. Self-catering holiday cottages are also available.

Verdict: A wonderful and unique bed & breakfast experience: Highly recommended

Rates Including Breakfast: Single from £50 ($85); Double or Twin Rooms from £75 ($125); Triple from £80 ($132).

Contact: Mount Pleasant Farm, Childswickham, Broadway, Worc. WR12 7HZ; Phone 01386 85342; Email helen@mountpleasantfarm.biz

Russell's

Following on from the last entry, Russell's has, since it open a few years ago, gained a reputation as one of the finest restaurants in the area, so say my relatives and friends that visit on a regular basis. Add Russell's Fish and Chip Shop just next at Number 20a, and you have the best of both worlds.

Fish & Chips is, of course, the English staple, and Russell's serve only the finest fish. You can eat in or take away, and the shop is open for Lunch and Dinner from 12noon-2.30pm and 5.00-8.30pm, Tuesday through Saturday – closed Sunday and Monday.

The **Swan Inn** at the north end of High Street, opposite the Village Green, offers good food at reasonable prices, as does the **Broadway Hotel** at the west side of the green.

If afternoon tea is what you're craving, well… you might like to try **Tisanes Tea Rooms** at Cotswold House on the Green where, so I'm told, Tracey and Steve will provide "a nice pot of tea or coffee with cakes, sandwiches and soft drinks.

Best Pubs

Nothing is more refreshing on warm summer day that a cool pint of local beer; better yet, nothing is more refreshing than an ice-cold pint of shandy – beer and lemonade mixed together in equal parts. Broadway has several nice pubs, including the **Broadway Hotel**, the **Swan Inn** and my favorite haunt, the **Horse and Hound** on upper High Street. Another of my old haunts is the **Crown and Trumpet** on Church Street, just off the Village Green on the left. It's been a while since I was last in there, but I have a feeling it's changed very little: great pint of beer, and quiet.

The trip includes Offenham, the Littletons, Bretforton and Wickhamford.

This is a fun and interesting sightseeing trip you'll not find in any other guide to the Cotswolds, though I often wonder why not. None of these delightful communities are classed as part of the Cotswolds, but they all have something special to offer, they are just on the edge of the Cotswolds and it's a lovely drive with lots to see and do along the way.

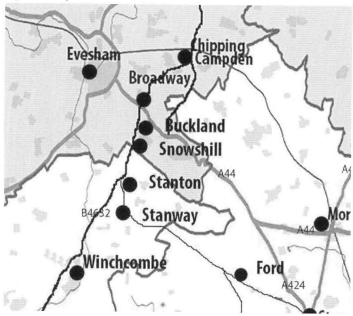

Map the Eastern Cotswold Villages and Towns

From Broadway, Chipping Campden or Winchcombe, it can be done as a half-day out. I recommend you start out around mid-morning and plan on being back at base camp in time for tea, around 4PM.

From Broadway to Evesham, the drive is just seven miles (15 minutes); from Chipping Campden, it's about 10 miles (25 minutes) and it's about the same from Winchcombe.

The entire round trip from Broadway will be no more than 24 miles, from Campden of Winchcombe 32 miles. From Broadway, take the A44 into Evesham; From Chipping Campden, take the B4081 west to the junction with the A44 and then drive on into Evesham; from Winchcombe, take the B4632 into Broadway and from there the A44 into Evesham.

Evesham

Evesham is a small market town in Worcestershire, just on the northern edge of the Cotswolds. The town was founded sometime during the end of the 7th Century, the late 600s. Over the past 100 years, or so, there's been quite a bit of controversy about how the town came by its name.

Sculpture of Eof - Photo Courtesy of Pat A. Marshall

It's not worth going into in depth here, but to most local folk Evesham is a derivative of the combination of two Old English words Eof and Homme (or Ham): Eof being the name of a swineherd in the service of Egwin, third bishop of Worcester and Homme meaning home, thus you would have the name Eof's Home or *Eveshomme* as recorded in 709. And as *Evesham* in 1086.

50

The legend tells us that Eof, while tending his pigs, had a vision of the Virgin Mary; Bishop Egwin is said to have built the great Benedictine Abbey at Evesham on that spot starting around the year 701. The Abbey was enlarged after the Norman Conquest and became one of the largest in England, but it fell victim to King Henry VIII's Dissolution of the abbeys and was demolished in 1540; only the great Bell Tower and parts of the abbey wall, including Cloisters Gateway remain; all are located in the Abbey Park and they alone are worth the visit.

Things to See in Evesham:

Abbot Clement Litchfield's Bell Tower

The Bell Tower dominates the Evesham skyline. It's an iconic structure built around 1530 to hold the bells of Evesham Abbey. The tower was commissioned by Abbot Clement Lichfield, the last abbot of Evesham. The Bell Tower is located close to where the north transept of the great Abbey Church once stood. The Church and almost all the monastic buildings were demolished in 1540 as part of the Dissolution by King Henry VIII. By all accounts, the Kings men entered the abbey during Evensong of January 30th. The monks were ejected and demolition began quickly after.

The Bell Tower by Moonlight – Copyright © Blair Howard

The Bell Tower survived the Dissolution; why is a matter of some conjecture: Some think it may have been because the people of Evesham had contributed to the cost of its construction; others will tell you it was a gift to the town from the King; some say that it was purchased from the King by the town for the sum of £100; the real reason is lost in the mists of time.

The Bell Tower in Daylight – Courtesy of Creative Commons

The Churchyard of All Saints and St. Lawrence

The Bell Tower today stands between the Abbey Churchyard and the Abbey Gardens, or Park, with an archway through the tower itself. The churchyard is unique in that it's the only one that I know of that contains two churches.

The Two Churches of St. Lawrence (left) and All
Saints – Copyright © Blair Howard

The two churches, St Lawrence and All Saints were
built by the Benedictine monks of Evesham Abbey in the
12th century to serve the people of Evesham. Abbot
Clement Lichfield is buried in the Church of All Saints.
Today, the two fine buildings, along with the adjacent
Abbot Reginald's Gateway, present a wealth of photo
opportunities.

Abbot Reginald's Gateway:

Abbot Reginald's Gateway is the walkway from the
town's market square into the churchyard of All Saints
and St. Lawrence and the Bell Tower and Abbey Park
beyond. Part of the gateway – the lower walls, date to
early Norman times; the upper buildings, probably 16th
century, once were the vicarage.

Abbot Reginald's Gateway – Copyright © Blair
Howard

Today, the gateway houses a tea room that bears the same name (lunch, afternoon tea and cakes) and a small antique shop. The Gateway, from both sides, presents a nice photo op, especially in winter when the snow is on the ground and the buildings.

The Almonry:

Located just outside the churchyard of All Saints and St. Lawrence churches, this 14th Century building was once home to the Almoner of the great Benedictine Abbey. The almoner of the abbey was the monk charged with looking after the poor and destitute of the town.

Following the Dissolution of the Abbey, the Almonry became the personal home of the abbot; whatever else was left of the Abbey buildings were sold to Sir Philip Hoby.

The Almonry and Stocks – Copyright © Blair Howard

The Almonry, over the past 475 years, has been many things to many people: a public house, tea rooms, even a private home. Finally, in 1929, the Almonry was purchased by Evesham Borough Council and, in 1957, it was opened to the public as a museum owned and funded by the Evesham town council and operated by the Vale of Evesham Historical Society.

Today the Almonry houses a wealth of information and artefacts, documenting such important happenings as the history of the great Abbey and the defeat of Baron Simon de Montfort at the Battle of Evesham in 1265. You can also view the abbot's great chair, a 14th century psalter (bible), and the famous Matthew Bible dated to 1537. The museum also houses relics from the Neolithic period to the present day, including Anglo-Saxon burial treasure, and artifacts from the Civil War.

The Abbey Park and Gardens and the Cloisters Arch:

The park and gardens are best accessed through Abbot Reginald's Gateway in the Market Place.

The Abbey Gardens-Courtesy Bill Johnson and
Creative Commons

You can view the two churches, walk through the arch under the Bell Tower, and on down to the riverbank. It's a nice, short walk and interesting too.

The Cloisters Arch – Copyright © Blair Howard

The Cloisters Arch is just to the right of the Bell Tower as you enter into the park from the churchyard, no more than 20 yards, or so. The arch dates to the 12th century and is interesting for its many carvings.

Best Pub:

One of my old favorites is the Royal Oak on Vine Street. The food is good and so is the beer.

The Royal Oak - Photo Courtesy of Pat A. Marshall

Ok, that's it for this section of the trip. From Evesham we drive a couple of miles to Offenham.

From Evesham, we'll drive about three miles to Offenham.

In Evesham, take Port Street south to Elm Road and bear left, then turn left on Offenham Road and drive on a couple of miles into Offenham.

By now, it's probably time for lunch and there are two pubs where we can do just that: The Bridge Inn and the Fish and Anchor. Both pubs are on the riverbank and both are nice places to take a short break.

My personal favorite is the Bridge Inn. I have spent countless weekend hours there: lunchtimes on Saturdays and Sundays, and Friday and Saturday evenings; it's just a very pleasant spot to sit back for a few minutes and relax over a sandwich and cool pint of beer. From Main Street, take Boat Lane to the Bridge Inn.

The Bridge Inn at Offenham – Courtesy of David Luther Thomas and Creative Commons

The Fish and Anchor does not have river access for boats, but it's also a nice place to eat lunch. You'll find it just out of Offenham on the B4510.

59

The Fish and Anchor – Copyright © Blair Howard

The view of the river is pleasant, and the food is good too.

Middle Little Tithe Barn

From Offenham, it's just a short drive of another three miles to Middle Littleton. Take the B4510 from Offenham, then turn left on Cleeve Road about 4/10 mile and turn left onto school lane and drive another 3/10 mile to the Tithe Barn and the Church.

The Tithe Barn is the main reason for this visit. It's one of the largest and certainly one of the finest 13th-century tithe barns in the country. It was built for the monks of Evesham Abbey, mostly of the local Cotswold stone. The barn measures some 130 feet in length and approximately 42 feet wide. This type of Tithe barn was used during the Middle Ages for storing the tithes received from the church's tenant farmers - a tenth of the farm's produce. In this case, Evesham Abbey.

The Great Tithe Barn at Middle Littleton – Courtesy of
Phillip Halling and Creative Commons

The National Record says that the Barn was built in
1376 by Abbot John Ombersley of Evesham, but the
National Trust, the organization that looks after the
building, gives the date as much earlier in the 13th
century, probably as result of radiocarbon testing that
dates the construction at around 1250.

The interior woodwork is amazing, especially the
hammer-beam truss-work supporting the roof. Middle
Littleton's Tithe barn truly is a magnificent building, and
a monument to the medieval craftsmen and engineers that
built it. The barn is open seven days a week.

The Interior of the Tithe barn Showing Construction
Details-Photo Courtesy of Creative Commons

The Church of St. Nicholas at Middle Littleton –
Courtesy of Phillip Halling and Creative Commons

St Nicholas' Church, situated between North and Middle Littleton parishes, is just a few yards walk from the Great Tithe barn, and it's worth a quick look while you're there.

Bretforton

The Fleece Inn at Bretforton is the next stop on our trip. Take the B4085 west to Blackminster and turn left onto Station Road and drive on into Bretforton, about 4 miles.

The Fleece Inn at Bretforton – Courtesy of Roger Davis and Creative Commons

Many's the pleasant evening I have spent supping a pint, or two, in the old Fleece Inn. This magnificent public house is more than 600 years old, and has been a pub since 1848. The inn was badly damaged by a fire in 2004, but has since been restored to its former glory and is now owned by the National Trust, which gives you some idea of how important the Fleece is considered to be.

Wickhamford

The final stop on the tour is Wickhamford. Take the B4035 Badsey-Bretforton road north out of Bretforton and turn right onto Badsey High Street, turn left onto

School Lane, then right onto Golden Lane, and then left on Manor Road.

The Manor House – Copyright © Blair Howard

The object of this trip is Wickhamford's tiny church, and its contents.

St John the Baptist Church, Wickhamford is located at the north of the village, next to the manor house.

Church of John the Baptist – Copyright © Blair Howard

Typical of most English country churches, the door of St. John the Baptist is usually open. You can simply walk inside and browse around undisturbed. Built early in the

12th century, it's an odd little Norman church with a tower instead of a steeple. When full, which it rarely is, it will seat maybe 60 people. There's no altar as such, just a fine antique table covered with a red velvet cloth. The vestments consist of a couple of candle sticks and a simple silver cross. The sanctuary is dominated by a magnificent, canopied monument to the Sandys family.

Sir Edwyn Sandys, a great English parliamentarian, was Treasurer of the Virginia Company during the reign of King James I, and it was through his influence that the first representative assembly in America met at Jamestown in 1619.

The Sandys Monument inside Wickhamford Church –
Copyright © Blair Howard

Other than the Sandys monument, there seems to be little else within the church to interest the visitor. But then, however, you might spot the small table just inside the main lobby. On it you will find a stack of small, informational booklets. These contain a brief history of the church. The booklet has only a half-dozen pages, and it's free. If you like, you can drop a small donation in the box provided. On the last page of that little book, in the second-to-last paragraph, you will learn that American visitors might be interested in the "floor-slab" monument located within the altar rails.

You would surely be forgiven for not spotting the slab sooner, for it's concealed beneath a large red rug that covers the floor beneath the altar table.

Step through the tiny gate in the altar rail - don't worry, no one will mind if you're careful - and pull back the rug, you will find a large stone slab set into the floor. It's perhaps six feet long by three feet wide.

The inscription on the slab is in Latin. It tells of the piety and virtue, and the generosity of the lady whose body lies beneath the slab, Penelope Washington. Penelope was the daughter of Colonel Henry Washington, a royalist hero of the English civil war. She also was a cousin the first American president, George Washington. Worth a visit? I think so, I hope you will too.

By the way, the village pub, The Sandys Arms, is famous for its "bar food," and the village itself is as pretty as they come, a fair ending to our day out.

From Wickhamford, it a drive of about three miles back to Broadway, say 10 miles to Chipping Campden or Winchcombe.

I placed Snowshill next on the list of places to visit after Broadway because it's no more than a hop-skip-and-a-jump away; well… two miles, or so.

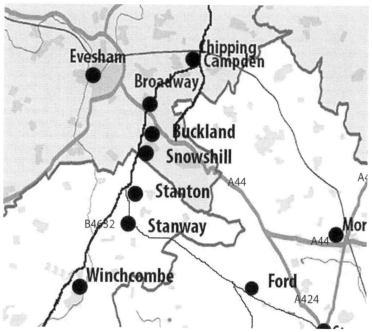

Map the Eastern Cotswold Villages and Towns

To reach Snowshill from Broadway, turn onto Church Street on the north side of the Green and drive two and a half miles up the hill into Snowshill, one of the most delightful and understated little villages in the Cotswolds.

Snowshill is not on any guided tour that I know of, but it certainly should be.

The Ice Cream Lady on the Roadside at Snowshill –
Copyright © Blair Howard

I remember the village when nobody visited, when the Snowshill Arms (the local pub) was almost derelict with a tree growing in the bar and pea sacks at the windows. In fact, I remember one Saturday evening when a friend and I were the only people in that bar; my how times do change.

Stone Cottages in Snowshill – Courtesy of Creative Commons

Snowshill is a typical example of the Cotswold village – honey-colored cottages with flowers out front, a single stone church and just one local pub and, like every other Cotswold village it has a unique personality and an appeal you just can't ignore. Snowshill is a seemingly remote little village with its ancient cottages and tiny church all clustered around a small village green. As close as it is to Broadway, it's well worth the short drive up the hill.

Things to See:

The Cotswold Lavender Farm

Here's an extraordinary experience for you. Snowshill Lavender is based just outside the village at Hill Barn Farm in Snowshill, and it's open to the public.

Cotswold Lavender Fields – Courtesy Mike Baldwin and Creative Commons

During the summer months, when the lavender is in flower, visitors are treated to an eye-popping rainbow of colors, and an all pervading assault on the olfactory senses, it smells really nice: 35 varieties of lavender spread over fifty-three acres.

Hill Barn Farm first started to grow lavender in 2000. The limestone soil is, apparently, ideal for growing the plants, and for producing the high quality essential oils they produce.

You can "walk through the lavender fields, taking in the scents and enjoying the peace and tranquility of the rolling hills. Then, of course, you'll want to visit the farm shop to browse "all things associated with the essence of lavender, plants and the other types of gifts."

Driving in from Broadway, as you enter the village, take the first road on the left then go left again to Cotswold Lavender.

Cotswold Lavender, Hill Barn Farm Snowshill, Broadway, Worcestershire, WR12 7JY; Phone 01386 854821.

St. Barnabus Church

St. Barnabus Church is not as old as it looks. Built in the Norman style in 1864, the tiny church is surrounded by its church yard and the village itself. It's probably one of the most photographed churches in the Cotswolds.

St. Barnabus Church – Courtesy Trevor Rickard and Creative Commons

Snowshill is, perhaps best known for its 15th century manor house, beautiful gardens and dovecote. Its roots go way back to the early-9th Century. During the years 821 to 1539, the property the manor house now stands upon was owned by Winchcombe Abbey.

That long period ended with the Dissolution of the Monasteries by King Henry VIII that same year. Between 1539 and 1919 it passed through several hands until it was finally purchased by Charles Wade, an avid collector of all things, artist, poet and craftsman. It seems though, Wade never did live in the manor House, preferring instead to occupy a small cottage in the Manor gardens; the big house he used to house his extensive collection of art, toys to suits of armour, musical instruments, clocks, furniture and a whole lot of items far too numerous to list here. In 1951, Wade gifted the property and his collection to the National Trust, the present day administrators of Snowshill Manor.

Snowshill Manor – Courtesy of Trover Rickard & Creative Commons

Snowshill Manor, Snowshill, near Broadway, WR12 7JU; Phone: 01386 852410; Email snowshillmanor@nationaltrust.org.uk

Opening hours are somewhat iffy, usually Wednesday through Sunday, closed on Mondays and Tuesdays, with some exceptions. It's best to call ahead if you'd like to visit the manor House.

The Snowshill Arms Pub

A typical old-world Cotswold pub with many of its original features still intact: exposed stone walls and beamed ceilings along with an open fireplace. The pub serves traditional ales from the Donnington brewery and offers traditional English pub food listed on a blackboard which is updated daily with a variety of specials

The Snowshill Arms – Courtesy of Stephen McKay and Creative Commons.

You can eat inside or outside in the beer garden, which has a large, play area for the kids. The Snowshill arms is a family-friendly pub; the views from the pub gardens over Buckland and Stanway are stunning.

The Snowshill Arms, Snowshill, Broadway, Worcestershire, WR12 7JU; Phone 01386 852653

From Broadway, head north on High Street toward Evesham and turn left on Cheltenham road, the B4632. Drive 1.2 miles toward Cheltenham and watch for the Buckland signpost, then turn left and drive on into the village.

Buckland is a beautiful, tree-shaded and secluded village nestled below Cotswolds escarpment at the foot of Burhill. Best known for its manor house, now a luxury hotel, its church, village green and for its rectory, thought to be the oldest in England; its impressive timbered hall dates from the fifteenth century.

Church of St. Michael – Courtesy Phillip Halling & Creative Commons

John Wesley, co-founder of the Methodist movement in England with his brother Charles, preached in the 13th Century church of St. Michael here in Buckland; who would have thought? Anyway, the church, surrounded by massive English oaks, is also famous for its east window of which contains some stunning 15th-century stained glass. The glass, "judged by some to be the nicest in the Cotswolds," is thought to have been taken from Hailes Abbey, just outside of Winchcombe, at the time of Dissolution of the Monasteries in 1539. William Morris, founder of the English Arts and Crafts Movement, attended church services at Buckland in the late 19th-century and was so impressed by the east window that he personally paid for its re-leading.

Buckland Manor Hotel:

Touted as one of the finest manor houses in the Cotswolds, and the home of Sir Richard Gresham, Lord Mayor of London in 1537, Buckland Manor House is now a luxury hotel; I wonder what the old boy would have thought of that. Be that as it may, the stately manor offers the ultimate in "gracious living and tradition, with the addition of all modern comforts and excellent service."

No, I haven't stayed therein, but I have visited the manor a couple of times, and it is all that it's made out to be. If you're looking for that oh-so-English country living experience, Buckland Manor is where you'll find it. In winter, you'll relax in front of a log fire, sleep in a four-poster bed in a guest bedroom that Henry VIII himself would have been proud to sleep in.

Buckland Manor Hotel - – Courtesy Phillip Halling &
Creative Commons

Facilities at Buckland manor include two beautifully
decorated lounges, one with old-world wood panelling
and a beamed ceiling, and three en-suite bedrooms all
furnished with luxury fittings and accessories. Room rates
per night range approximately from £195 (300) for a
double/twin room to £470 ($730) for the Master King
room. All rates include a full English breakfast.

Buckland Manor, Nr Broadway, Worcestershire,
England, WR12 7LY; Phone 01386 852626.

Email info@bucklandmanor.co.uk

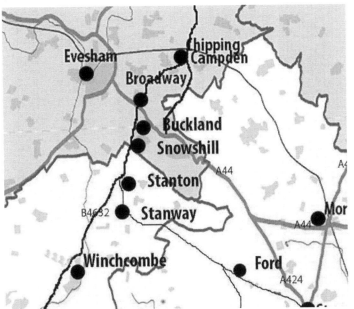

Map the Eastern Cotswold Villages and Towns

Stanton is another small village, not far from Broadway, just off the Broadway to Cheltenham road. During my youth, I spent more time in Stanton than anywhere else in the Cotswolds, and much of it at the local pub, the Mount Inn located at the far end of the village.

Stanton is one of the prettiest villages in the Cotswolds, little changed in more than 300 years. The overall feeling of timelessness is enhanced by the silence. Usually, the only sounds to be heard or those of the birds singing and the occasional clip-clop of horse and rider making for the slopes of Shenbarrow Hill. The ancient houses, most of them dating to the 16th and 17th Centuries, are typical of the Cotswolds, built from the local stone, and they literally glow in the afternoon sunshine.

Main Street Stanton – Courtesy of Dave Bushell and
Creative Commons

Stanton is a sleepy little village. There are no shops, restaurants and cafés here, just the visually pleasing main street, the Mount pub set on a mound on the hillside with stunning views across the Vale of Evesham, the Malvern Hills and, on a clear day, the Welsh mountains.

Other features in the village worthy of a mention are medieval cross and the Norman church of St. Michael and All Angels – just look at the amazing interior of the church:

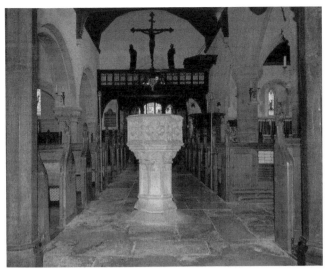

Church of St. Michael and All Angels, Stanton –
Courtesy W. Lloyd MacKenzie and Creative Commons

Again, as Stanton is as close as it is to Broadway, I strongly urge you take time out to visit this picturesque little village. If you can, arrive in time for lunch at the Mount Inn, sit a while on the terrace and enjoy those spectacular views.

Best Pub

The only pub in Stanton is the Mount, and I can recommend it heartily.

The Mount Inn at Stanton – Courtesy of Dave Bushell and Creative Commons

From Broadway, head north on High Street toward Evesham and turn left on Cheltenham road, the B4632. Drive 2.5 miles toward Cheltenham and watch for the Stanton signpost, then turn left and drive on into the village.

Where to Stay:

Want to stay the night in Stanton? Try the Vine, a small guest house and, as far as I know the only one in the village. The Vine is run by an old friend of mine, Jill Carenza. She also runs a riding stable on the property so, if you fancy going horseback riding through the village and up into the hills, you might want to give her a call: Jill Carenza, The Vine, Stanton, Near Broadway, Worcestershire, WR12 7NE; Phone 01386 584250; Fax: 01386 584888

Leave Stanton by way of the tiny road that runs past The Vine and go about two miles and you will arrive in the tiny village of Stanway.

The Massive Gatehouse at Stanway House – Courtesy of John Sparshatt & Creative Commons

The interest here is Stanway House. A Jacobean mansion built in the 16th century. The great house and its massive, three-story gate-house are said to be the work of Inigo Jones. In 2004 a water garden was added to the property. It features what is claimed to be the highest fountain in Britain; the single jet of water rises to 300 feet.

Stanway House – Courtesy of Derek Bennett &
Creative Commons

The Tithe Barn at Stanway House – Courtesy of David
Stowell & Creative Commons

The manor, water garden and great tithe-barn are open
to the public on Tuesdays and Thursdays from 2pm until
5pm, June, July and August; the entrance fee is £7 for
adults and £2 for children under the age of 14.

Time for afternoon tea? You've got to try the Old
Bakehouse Tearoom. A traditional Cotswold Tearoom

serving delicious homemade 'Cream Teas', homemade cakes with a pot of tea or coffee. The Old Bakehouse, Stanway, GL54 5PH; 01386 584204. The Tearoom is open on Tuesday, Thursday and Sunday from 2pm until 4.45pm.

Return to the B4632 turn left and head toward Cheltenham for about five miles and you come to the old market town of Winchcombe. You'll pass the turn for Hailes Abbey about a mile-and-a-half before you reach the town limits. If you want to visit on your way in, fine, but it's not far and you can catch it on your way back.

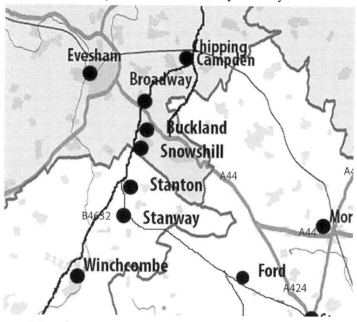

Map the Eastern Cotswold Villages and Towns

If you'd like a really interesting experience, check out the time tables in Broadway and do the round-trip to Winchcombe by bus. It's fun and it's a great way to see the sights along the way. Visitors to Cheltenham can do the same.

Winchcombe High Street – Courtesy of Andrew Smith & Creative Commons

Winchcombe is a busy little town. Parking space is scarce, and at a premium. It's a tiny, old-world town with a long and narrow main street, a dozen, or so, small and even narrower side streets and, of course, Sudeley Castle.

The Corner Cupboard Pub – Courtesy of Stanley Walker & Creative Commons

It's picturesque, historic, and well worth a visit. Sudeley Castle especially so. I have spent many a sunny, Sunday afternoon in the gardens at Sudeley. Not only is it one of the most peaceful spots in the Cotswolds, it's also one of the most photographed.

Castle Street – Courtesy of Andrew Smith & Creative Commons

Best Pubs

Time for lunch, or even a pint of real ale? Well, you have at least a dozen attractive options, from the White Heart Inn on the High Street, to the Corner Cupboard Inn, and the Plaster's Arms.

Dent Terrace and the Plasterer's Arms (white building)
– Courtesy of Graham Horn & Creative Commons

Just for food, there are several small tea rooms, and you can also eat in the concessions area at Sudeley Castle – not my personal choice, but good enough.

Vineyard Walk Winchcombe © Blair Howard

Winchcombe's roots go all the way back to Saxon times, long before the Norman Conquest, and are closely linked to the Benedictine abbey founded in the 8th century by King Cenwulf of Mercia who reigned from

796 to 821. The abbey at Winchcombe suffered many a downfall before it was finally destroyed by Lord Seymore of Sudeley in 1539 during the Dissolution of the Monasteries ordered by King Henry VIII. Nothing of that abbey now remains.

Sudeley Castle, however, does remain - at least most of it does. The town contains many ancient and interesting houses and inns but it's Sudley Castle that will take your breath away.

What to See:

Sudeley Castle

Sudeley Castle, owned by Lady Elizabeth Ashcombe, formerly of Lexington, Kentucky, also dates back beyond the Norman Conquest, to the 9th Century when, in one form or another, it belonged to King Ethelred the Unready.

Photo Courtesy of Michael Reeve & Creative Commons

The estate was, "highly prized being rich in oaks and included a royal deer park." Ethelred granted the estate to his daughter Goda, a sister of King Edward the Confessor. After the Norman Conquest the estate passed to her son Ralph de Sudeley and then to his son John de Sudeley who was Lord Chamberlain to King Edward II. The estate was then passed on to one Ralph Le Boteler, an Admiral of the Fleet who fought the French under King Henry V. He was created Baron Sudeley in 1441. Boteler, suspected of being a traitor during the Wars of the Roses, was reluctantly forced to sell the castle to the king in 1469. He died without an heir in 1469.

Photo Courtesy of Saffron Blaze & Creative Commons

The castle was then owned briefly by an assortment of court favorites culminating with Richard, Duke of Gloucester who was later to become King Richard III. When Richard died on Bosworth Field in 1495 the castle became the property of King Henry VII and subsequently of King Henry VIII in 1509. When King Henry died 1548 the boy king, Edward VI, gave the castle and its estates to his uncle, Sir Thomas Seymour. Seymour was the brother of Henry VIII's third wife, Jane Seymour and he was "the most attractive and prominent man of his day."

When Henry died Lord Seymour set his cap at the king's last wife, Queen Katherine Parr who, before her marriage to Henry, had been his lover. Thomas Seymour and Katherine Parr were married only weeks after Henry VIII's death.

Photo Courtesy of Jason Ballard & Creative Commons

Sir Thomas Seymour took his bride to Sudeley accompanied by the infamous Lady Jane Grey who lived with Katherine and several hundred other members of the royal household, including ladies-in-waiting, maids of honor, gentlemen of the household and yeomen of the guard, until the dowager queen died the following year. Queen Katherine is buried in the St. Mary's Chapel in the Castle grounds.

Sir Thomas Seymour was executed for treason 1549 and the castle was granted to the first Lord Chandos by Queen Mary in 1554.

Civil war broke out in England in 1642 and George Bryges, 6th Lord Chandos, allied himself to King Charles I (big mistake). Sudeley Castle became the Royalist headquarters under the king's dashing young nephew, Prince Rupert.

On January 27 1643, during the absence of Lord Chandos, the castle surrendered to the parliamentary forces under the command of the Earl of Essex. The castle was plundered and the church desecrated. King Charles was able to re-take the castle, but in June of 1644 it was surrendered once again. Oliver Cromwell ordered the fortress "neutralized" and much of it was laid to ruin. Even so, one can still see much of the castle's former glory in the ruins of the great banqueting hall.

St. Mary's Chapel and Gardens - Courtesy of Jason
Ballard & Creative Commons

At the end of the war Lord Chandos was heavily fined
and only was able to retain his home by defecting his
allegiance to the now executed King Charles. Lord
Chandos died in disgrace of smallpox in 1655.

There followed many years of neglect until the castle
was taken over by the Dent family in 1837. Emma Dent-
Brocklehurst began the restoration of the castle in the
mid-1800s, and it is to this lady that much of the credit
must go for the fine condition of the castle today. Emma
died in 1900 and the castle has remained in the Dent-
Brocklehurst family ever since.

View from the ruins of the Tithe Barn to the castle –
Copyright © Blair Howard

Today visitors can wander through the public rooms of
the castle at will, for a small fee, of course. It is a strange
individual indeed who can stand among the relics of the
castle's great past and remain unaffected. Queen
Katherine's rooms remain intact, much as they were when,
almost 500 years ago, she must have swept along the
narrow passageways with her retinue hurrying along in
close pursuit.

Queen Katherine's Tomb in St. Mary's Chapel at
Sudeley Castle – Courtesy of Saffron Blaze & Creative
Commons

Then, of course, there are the gardens, and oh what
gardens they are. Laid out along formal lines, the Queen's
Garden is one of my favorite spots in the Cotswolds. On a
summer's day the air seems, at least to me, usually heavy
and still, the quiet solitude of the gardens is, I think, an
unworldly experience.

Some years ago, I interviewed Lord and Lady
Ashcombe at length. It was a while ago, but I remember
well these words from Lady Ashcombe, "There is such a
texture of life here. You can feel all that has evolved. It's
not a haunting feeling but it's a feeling of continuity of

life of a thousand years. Yet the checkered nature of its past has meant that, unlike an ancestral home, the castle has relied on the chance dedication of individuals for its continued survival."

The Queen's Garden at Sudeley Castle – Copyright © Blair Howard

You can tour the public room and view many important paintings, including John Constable, Anthony van Dyck and Peter Paul Ruebens to name just a few.

You'll step backward through the ages when you visit the bedroom of Katherine Parr, and wonder at the prayer-book, and the love-letter she wrote to Lord Seymore in the year of her husband's death. And you can visit her final resting place in the private chapel of St. Mary, surrounded by the castle gardens. You can also tour the beautiful formal gardens, take time out for afternoon tea and sit for a moment or two and wonder at the castle's history. A visit to Sudeley is a visit to remember.

Sudeley Castle is open to the public from April to end of October. Daily from 10.30am to 5.00pm. Adults £7.20. Children 5-15yrs: £4.20. Children under 5: Free. Family Ticket (2 Adults, 2 Children): £20.80. Members & Friends of the Historic Houses Association: Free www.sudeleycastle.co.uk Sudeley Castle, Winchcombe, nr. Cheltenham, Gloucestershire, GL54 5JDVisitor Centre: 01242 604244

Hailes Abbey:

The Cistercian abbey of Hailes was founded in 1246 in Gloucestershire, just outside of Winchcombe, by Richard, Earl of Cornwall in thanks for surviving a shipwreck. It was and dissolved Christmas Eve 1539.

The Ruins of the Abbey at Hailes– Courtesy of Bill Tyne & Creative Commons

Richard was the younger brother of King Henry III who granted the manor of Hailes to Richard. After surviving the shipwreck, he gave the manor to the Cistercian Order and thus the Abbey at Hailes came into being. The abbey was consecrated in 1277 with a royal ceremony that included the King, Queen and 15 bishops.

Hailes never was a large community, but it became a very rich one, thanks to its ownership of a much renowned holy relic, 'the Holy Blood of Hailes.' Claimed by the abbey monks to be a phial of Christ's own blood taken at the Crucifixion, it was donated to the Cistercian community by Richard's son Edmund, and denounced by

King Henry VIII's commissioners and declared a fake in 1536.

The Ruins of the Abbey at Hailes - – Courtesy of
Saffron Blaze & Creative Commons

In an effort to save the abbey from the Dissolution, the then Abbot Stephen Sagar admitted that the Holy Blood was indeed a fake. It was not to be, Abbot Sagar and his monks finally surrendered their abbey to Henry's commissioners on Christmas Eve 1539.

Today, little remains of the once magnificent abbe, just a few of the cloister arches and a one of the most beautiful picnic spots in the Cotswolds. So, when in Winchcombe, I strongly urge you to take a little time and visit this lovely public site. You can visit the small museum, and "bring the abbey to life with our vivid interpretation panels and free audio tour and see site finds in the museum. Imagine how the monks and lay brothers once lived, ate and slept, and see the clever Cistercian drain which still works after 750 years."

The Church at Hailes – Courtesy of Phillip Halling & Creative Commons

The Hailes Abbey site is maintained and managed by English Heritage, and owned by the National Trust.

The Cistercian abbey at Hailes is two miles northeast of Winchcombe on the B4632.

Belas Knap

Belas Knap, an important restored Stone Age burial mound, lies southeast of Winchcombe. If you have the time, and can manage the two-mile walk up the hill (well, thereabouts), it's well worth a visit.

The Long Barrow at Belas Knap – Courtesy Nigel
Homer and Creative Commons

The barrow is about 178 feet long, about 60 feet wide
and nearly 14 feet high. The main entrance to the barrow,
with its fancy dry-stone walling is a modern addition: the
actual burial chambers are down the long East and West
sides of the barrow and at its Southern end. There are six
burial chambers, two on either side near the center, one at
the south-cast angle and one at the south end.

The long barrow was first excavated 1863 to 1865
when the skeletal remains of five children and a young
adult male were found, along with an assortment of
animal bones and fragments of pottery and flint tools
were found. Further excavations in 1963 revealed the
remains of 38 more human skeletons, together with
animal bones, flint implements and pottery all dating
roughly to the Neolithic period – the New Stone Age,
2,000 BC.

How to Get There:

This peaceful, and very beautiful spot can be reached
by either of two paths. The best, and most well-known, is
the steep and narrow Charlton Abbots road (Corndean
Lane) just to the south of Winchcombe. Take the B4632
for about a half mile then turn left up the hill. There's a
'pull-in' on the left, with a Cotswold Way signpost
pointing up through the trees to the right. It's quite a steep
climb, but the views of Winchcombe are breathtaking.

The White Hart Inn is a charming 16th Century inn
that offers hotel and bed & breakfast accommodation in
the heart of Winchcombe which is a small historic town
set in the Cotswold countryside just outside the famous
spa town of Cheltenham.

Where to Stay; Where to Eat:

There's not a whole lot of opportunities in
Winchcombe, other than the obvious B&Bs. Of the local

inns, I can recommend a couple: The Wesley House Hotel and the White Heart.

The Wesley House Hotel

The Wesley House is a small hotel on the High Street. The rates are reasonable and the rooms are comfortable and appealing. The rates start at £65 for a small single rising to £205 for a Terrace room – double occupancy.

The restaurant at the Wesley House is somewhat formal and serves "modern European food in an elegant yet relaxed setting." If you'd like something a little more laid-back, you can eat at the bar and grill next door; it's also owned by the Wesley House.

Wesley House, High Street, Winchcombe, Glos., GL54 5LH; Phone 01242 602366;

The White Heart Inn:

The White Hart Inn is offers eight "individually styled" guest rooms, all en-suite rooms, and three smaller rooms with "shared facilities." The three small rooms can also be used as a family suite. The inn will provide bed and breakfast and half board.

The restaurant offers British dishes created using local ingredients, when possible, and is open breakfast, morning coffee and cakes, lunch and bar snacks, afternoon teas and dinner and, of course, a good old pint of best, or a glass of wine.

Naunton is a tiny village way off the beaten path about four miles from Bourton-on-the-Water; seemingly in another world. Naunton is a delight and one you shouldn't miss. It's just four miles from Winchcombe and Sudeley Castle, and five miles from Stow-on-the-Wold.

From Sudeley Castle you will turn right, follow Campden Lane up the hill, and drive for about five or six miles, through Guiting Power and down into the tiny village of Naunton.

From Stow on the Wold, you'll take the B4068 to Naunton, about 5 miles.

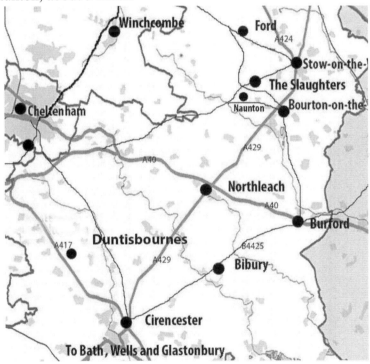

Map of South Central Cotswolds

Naunton - Courtesy of Julian Dowse & Creative
Commons

Take a couple of moments to look at the mill stream
and the gardens. The 17th-century dove-cote that stands
in the manor yard is also worth a stop on your way
through.

The Dovecote at Naunton - Courtesy of Pam Brophy &
Creative Commons

The village is set along the banks of the tiny River Windrush. This is, indeed "chocolate box cover country." The tiny church with its beautiful tower with pinnacles and gargoyles features a fine, early 15th-century carved stone pulpit and font. Photo ops include the little bridge over the River Windrush, the church, the Old Rectory and, of course, the beautiful gardens. Naunton is a place where you can decide, on a whim, to stay the night, or maybe a couple of nights, and enjoy some stunning country walks.

Best Pub:

The Black Horse is a Donnington house and I've spent many a lunch time and evening therein. Real ale and good food.

The Black Horse Pub at Naunton – Courtesy of Stephen McKay & Creative Commons

Where to Stay:

Foxhill

A lovely old Cotswold home that once was a coaching inn, is just about as nice a Cotswold B&B as you will find. If you're looking for local Naunton charm, peace and tranquility, you'll find it at Foxhill. As I mentioned earlier, this would be a great place to spend a couple of days enjoying the country walks around the village.

All of the guest room feature exposed beams and stonework, and stunning views over the countryside. All have tea/coffee making facilities, TVs, hairdryer, fresh flowers and magazines. Internet access and Wi-Fi are available on request.

Contact:

Foxhill Bed & Breakfast, Old Stow Road, Naunton, Glos, GL54 5RL; Phone 01451 850496

Stow-on-the-Wold

Stow-on-the-Wold is a small, Cotswold market town situated at the junction of seven major roads through the Cotswolds, including the Fosse Way (the A429). The Fosse Way is built on the foundation of the Roman Road of the same name.

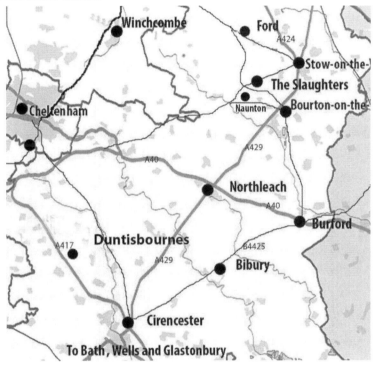

Map of South Central Cotswolds

I'm sorry, but I have to tell you, Stow-on-the-Wold never was a favorite of mine. Having said that, I have visited the town many, many times, and I do know that it's an extremely popular visitor destination. Why is it not a favorite of mine? Well, I always found it a little too commercial for my taste, but there you go.

Stow-on-the-Wold today is an important stop on the tourist map and, during spring and summer, you can bet it will be very busy. It's a major shopping center where you can browse dozens of art galleries, gift shops, crafts shops and antique shops.

The Market Cross in the Market Square – Courtesy of David Stowell and Creative Commons

Stow as it is today has its roots in the late 12th Century, after the Norman Conquest. The town, then known as Edwardstow after the town's patron saint, Edward the Confessor, was granted a market charter in 1107 by King Henry I, the younger son of William the Conqueror and market fairs have been held in Stow by royal charter since 1330; an annual horse fair is still held today on the edge of the town

But Stow has an even longer history: it is said to have originated as an Iron Age fort on this defensive position on a hill. Indeed, it seems that most villages and towns in the Cotswolds have similar roots: there are number of such sites in the area, including Stone Age and Bronze Age forts, settlements and burial mounds.

The "Market" was an important part of the economy both in Norman times and even today. Edward III, in 1330, called for an annual seven-day market to be held each August. Edward IV in 1476, expanded on the theme with two 5-day fairs, two days before and two days after the feast of St Philip and St James in May, and also in October on the feast of St Edward the Confessor.

The Market Hall - Courtesy of Graham Horn and Creative Commons

The fairs were held in the market square at the center of the town. When the wool industry was at its peak in the Cotswolds, it was not unusual 20,000, or even more, sheep to be brought to market. The Market Square at Stow is a testament to the town's importance to the Cotswold wool industry.

Stow in the mid-1600s was not a place you would have wanted to be. During the English Civil War, 1642 to 1646 and 1648 to1649, several small battles and skirmishes to place in and around the town, including one that resulted in significant damage to the church of St. Edward.

The end of the troubles came for Stow when, on 21 March 1646, the Royalists, commanded by Sir Jacob Astley, were defeated at the Battle of Stow-on-the-Wold, a major confrontation and the final battle of the first Civil War. Apparently, upwards of 1,000 Royalist prisoners were locked up in the Church of St. Edward. You should visit St. Edwards church and view the monument to Sir Hastings Keyte, who was a Royalist Captain killed in the battle. He was just 23 years old. The entrance to the church is also worthy of note, as you can see in the photo.

The Church of St. Edward - Square – Courtesy of John Salmon and Creative Commons

The Main Door to the Church of St. Edward, guarded by two ancient yew trees – Courtesy of Martyn Gorman and Creative Commons

And so Stow began a long period of economic growth that still continues today. Although the sheep are long gone, the fairs continue and include horse sales, crafts, antiques and, so I understand, a whole lot of partying.

A Quiet Corner of the Market Square Courtesy of
Robin Drayton and Creative Commons

There are several nice restaurants, cafes and some
really fine pubs. Stow is also a major stop for hikers along
the Cotswold Way.

Best Pubs:

Stow is also home to what is claimed to be the second
oldest pub in England, the Eagle and Child, which has
been serving beer since the early 10th century. Today, the
pub is actually more hotel than pub with a small bar that
features flagstone floors and low beams. The food is very
good and the beer is very drinkable – Brakespears, Oxford
Gold, etc. Children and dogs are welcome; seating
includes picnic tables out front, and there's a small
courtyard at the rear. See the photo:

Photo Courtesy of David Stowell and Creative
Commons

How to get there:

Stow-on-the-Wold is easily reached from Broadway, Chipping Campden or Cheltenham, all are just a short 30-minute drive away. From Chipping Campden, take the A424; from Broadway, take the A44 to the junction with the A424; from Cheltenham, take the A40 through Charlton Kings to the junction with the A429 at Northleach, turn left and drive on into Stow.

Where to Stay:

Stow Lodge Hotel

An AA three-star rated hotel situated in the heart of the Cotswolds, Stow Lodge is a hotel I know quite well, and I have no hesitation in recommending as a great place to stay and, if need be, your base camp for your visit to the area; it's quite close to all the major attractions – Broadway, Chipping Campden, Bourton-on-the-Water, Chedworth, etc. Family-owned by Dave and Val Hartley, and surrounded by beautiful gardens, it's a peaceful spot to spend your vacation.

Stow Lodge – Courtesy of Chris Hartley

All Bedrooms are en-suite and have televisions, beverage making facilities, hairdryer, direct dial telephone, electric fans and radios. Some rooms have double beads, some king beds, and one even has a four-poster bed. Expect to pay: From £75 in the low season to £109.00 high Season.

Contact: Stow Lodge Hotel, the Square, Stow-on-the-Wold, Cheltenham, Gloucestershire, GL54 1AB; Phone 01451 830485 Fax 01451 831671 enquiries@stowlodge.com; http://www.stowlodge.co.uk/

The Old Stocks Hotel

The Old Stocks Hotel is a Grade II Listed building dating back to the 16th century located on Stow's Market Square with a view out over the green where the "the old stocks" still stand. Owned and operated by Jason and Helen Allen, the hotel offers "all the home comforts. The décor is tasteful and sympathetic to the period, while at the same time every modern convenience is provided for your comfort and pleasure."

All rooms are en-suite and have central heating, televisions, direct dial telephones, tea/coffee making facilities. Better yet, the hotel has on-site laundry facilities and a private car park. Expect to pay from £70.00 to £130.00 per night.

Contact: Old Stocks Hotel, The Square, Stow on the Wold, Gloucestershire, GL54 1AF; Phone 01451 830666; Fax 01451 870014; info@oldstockshotel.co.uk http://www.oldstockshotel.co.uk/

Corsham Field Farmhouse

A charming, countryside just one-and-a-half miles from Stow-on-the-Wold, Corsham Field is a quiet and peaceful place to stay with stunning views of the surrounding hills and pastoral countryside. Beautiful gardens, country walks and its close proximity to Stow, make it a good choice if you're planning on making Stow your base in the Cotswolds.

Photo Courtesy of Corsham Field Farmhouse

All the bedrooms are centrally heated, have tea tray, TV and hairdryer with either en-suite or private bathroom, plus it's a smoke free environment. The Farm House is open all year for bed and English breakfast and even offers special rates for longer stays.

Contact: Corsham Field Farmhouse, Bledington Road, Stow-on-the-Wold, Gloucestershire GL54 1JH; Phone 01451 831750; Fax 01451 831750; Email farmhouse@corshamfield.co.uk.

Bourton-on-the-Water, one of the Cotswolds' most visited destinations, is a personal favorite of mine. I, literally, could not even hazard a guess as to how many times I've visited this quaint, old-world and visually appealing little town. My mother used to take me when I was a small child, I used to take my own children, and I still visit when Bourton whenever I can.

Bourton-on-the-Water is just 4 miles from Stow-on-the-Wold: take the A429 (the Fosse Way) west for four miles and turn right.

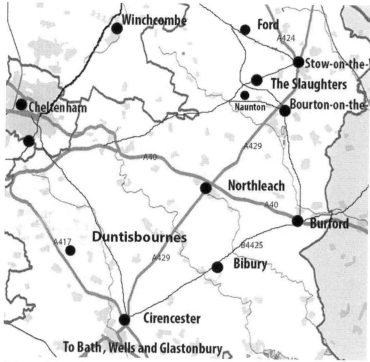

Map of South Central Cotswolds

The River Windrush - Courtesy of Keith Fairhurst and
Creative Commons

Bourton-on-the-Water is named for the tiny river upon which it sits. The river Windrush is a delightful little waterway, a tinkling brook or creek that runs directly through the center of town. Along the way, a series of picturesque, low stone bridges provide access to the shops and cafes on one side or the other. The riverbank is lined trees, neatly trimmed lawns and honey-colored Cotswold stone banks.

All of the buildings that line the streets are built from the same honey-colored stone, most of them dating back to the 17th Century. Many of the old homes remain while others have been converted into small, intimate shops and restaurants. Bourton, today, is an important center for tourism and, sadly, perhaps a little more commercial than many of the villagers would like. Even so, the villagers do their best to make Bourton a fun place to visit

Cotswold Stone Cottages in Bourton-on-the-Water - Courtesy of David Barnes and Creative Commons.

Bourton-on-the-Water Attractions

The main attraction, at least for me, is the river Windrush. To sit and watch the water tinkling by on warm summer afternoon is a treat; to walk the riverbanks at sunset, or even sunrise, is a rare treat, and to enjoy the waterside view along with a pint of local beer at the Old Manse pub is a treat I could not begin to describe. Try it. I think you'll agree.

The River Windrush at Bourton-on-the-Water –
Courtesy of Saffron Blaze and Creative Commons

Birdland

Birdland Park and Gardens, established by Len Hill, is home of some 600 species of birds, including a remarkable collection of penguins. There's also and a large pond full of fish – yes, you can feed them – the staff also present Birds of Prey and penguin feeding. It's a fun place to visit; many of the birds are allowed to fly loose among the trees.

King Penguins at Birdland Courtesy of Christine
Matthews and Creative Commons

The Model Village

The Model Village, one of the most popular of Bourton's attractions, is located behind the Old New Inn. The model, built by local craftsmen in the 1930s, and opened in 1937, is an exact replica of Bourton-on-the-Water. It's built of natural Cotswold stone to one-ninth scale. For a small fee, you can become Gulliver for a day and wander the streets of this miniature village at will.

The Model Village - Courtesy of Adrian Pingstone and Creative Commons

Other attractions include a perfume factory and model railway exhibition.

Bourton is also the confluence of several long-distance walks, including the Cotswold Way, and the Heart of England Way, a 100-mile hike that actually finishes in the village.

Best Pub:

The Mousetrap Inn

With a name like that, how could it not be a great pub? Well, it is, and I can recommend it. They serve good old English "pub grub." and local English ales. Pub Grub? In this case it means they still serve the traditional Ploughman's lunch in the summer time and good hot stews and puddings in the winter. Yes, you can get a steak if you want - vegetarians are also catered for - and breakfast is available each morning; dinner is served Tuesday through Saturday.

. Where to Stay:

Southlands Bed and Breakfast

Southlands is an old-world country house set amid beautifully landscaped gardens in Bourton on the Water. A non-smoking house where you can enjoy bed and breakfast – the Full English option or the continental breakfast; vegetarians are also catered for - and an evening meal is available should you so desire. The establishment is comfortable and inviting with 5 en-suite guest rooms. All rooms televisions and tea/coffee making facilities. Wi-Fi is also available.

Prices start from: £55.00 per double room with single occupancy; £75.00 per double room; £85.00 per family room. Note the rates quoted are subject to change on weekends, holidays any special events

Contact: Southlands, Rissington Road, Bourton-on-the-Water, Gloucestershire GL54 2DT; Phone 01451 821987;; Email info@southlands-bb.co.uk

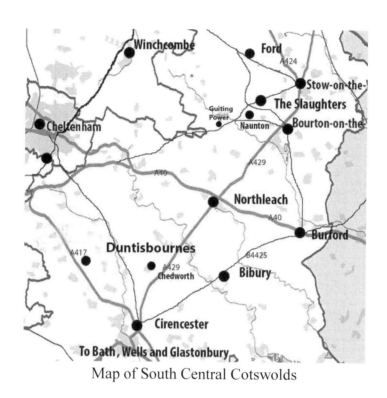
Map of South Central Cotswolds

Guiting Power is a tiny village set seemingly in the middle of nowhere between Bourton-on-the-Water and Winchcombe. As with most of these hilltop villages, Guiting Power has its roots set deep in pre-history. There is evidence of a late Anglo-Saxon settlement on this site, and there's no doubt that, with its proximity to the River Windrush, there must have been a settlement here long before that. Guiting Power is a small cluster of expensive honey colored cottages set close to a tributary of the river Windrush, with a post office, a small shop, bakery, two churches, and two pubs grouped around a village green.

Photo Courtesy of Creative Commons

This is walking country. From the village to the Cotswold Farm Park, it's a delightful walk of about 60 minutes. Or you can go northwest to Guiting Woods - absolutely a stunning walk - or southeast along the valley to Naunton.

How to Get There:

From either Winchcombe or Bourton-on-the-Water, take the B4068 and drive about six miles: the village is roughly mid-way between the two.

Best Pubs:

The Farmers Arms

Photo Courtesy of Steve Bennett and Creative Commons

On old world Cotswold pub with flagstone floors, a log fire during the winter months, great food - home cooked by the landlord - Donnington beers, and real English pub atmosphere. The service is friendly and efficient, the menu is displayed the old fashioned way, on a blackboard and includes such goodies as burgers, cottage pie, and rabbit pie. There's a nice garden, a skittle alley, and children welcome, but no B&B. And yes, I've spent many a happy hour here at the Farmers.

Hollow Bottom Inn: See below

Bed & Breakfast:

Hollow Bottom Inn:

If ever there was a stereotypical English/Cotswold pub, this is it, and that's a good thing. The interior has a large fireplace wood beams and lots of atmosphere. Hollow Bottom is one of the Cotswolds' better B&Bs, I think: good food, especially breakfast, and clean comfortable rooms. The service is excellent, the staff friendly and helpful, and its location on the road to Winchcombe is prime, and yes... the beer is good too. If you're looking for a great place to spend a night, or two, you should consider the Hollow Bottom Inn.

Rates: Expect to pay upward of £70 ($110) per night, depending upon the day of the week, and the season.

Contact: The Hollow Bottom, Guiting Power, Cheltenham, Gloucestershire, GL54 5UX; Telephone: 01451 850392, Fax: 01451 850945, Email: hello@hollowbottom.com

Things to See:

Photo Courtesy of Peter Vardy and Creative Commons

The church of St. Michael just to the south of the village dates from the 12th century. Of the original Norman building, only two doorways remain, the chancel is still 12th century, but was added somewhat later. The church is built from Cotswold limestone, including the slate roofs, also limestone. The church we see today is a cruciform layout consisting of a nave, north and south transepts, a west tower, and a chancel with a north vestry.

Near Guiting Power is the Cotswolds Farm Park with many interesting breeds of animal and is a favorite destination of families.

Cotswold Farm Park:

Located less than three miles from the village, the Cotswold Farm Park is home to "Britain's most comprehensive collection of rare breeds of British farm animals." And even though it's one of the Cotswolds' premier tourist attractions, it's still very much a working farm. Be that as it may, there's plenty to see and do for visitors of all ages, but especially for the kids: rabbits, guinea pig, lambs, baby goats, piglets, calves, a ride around the complex on a farm tractor and trailer, and a whole host of farming demonstrations to enjoy, including (depending upon the season, and time of day) lambing, shearing and milking. It's a fun couple of hours and one you shouldn't miss.

Opening Hours: From February to December, the park is open seven days a week from 10:30am. Closing hours vary depending upon the season.

Admission: Adults £8.50; Children £7.50 (under 3 free); Family up to four £30

Contact: Cotswold Farm Park Limited, Guiting Power, Nr. Cheltenham, Glos. GL54 5UG; **Phone** 01451-850307; **Website:**http://cotswoldfarmpark.co.uk/; **Email:**info@cotswoldfarmpark.co.uk

Ford

You'll not find this one in any other guide book, and I include here only because of its excellent pub, the Plough, within which I have spent many a pleasant evening, consumed many a fine meal, and downed many pints of fine Donnington ale.

The Hamlet of Ford - Courtesy of Norman Hyett and Creative Commons

Ford is a tiny Cotswold hamlet just a couple of miles or so from Stanway and only one mile from Temple Guiting on the B4077. Just a small collection of cottages and a pub on the upper reaches of the River Windrush. There's not a whole lot to see and do there, but the Plough Inn alone is well worth making the short drive from any one of the surrounding Cotswold villages; I would even say it's worth making the trip from London just to experience the food, which is out of this world.

Best Pubs

The Plough Inn

The Plough is a popular 16th Century Inn widely renowned for its excellent cuisine and, of course, its fine Donnington Ales.

The Plough Inn at Ford

The Restaurant:

My personal favorite is the slow roasted half shoulder of lamb with mint jelly, but I can also recommend the Plough's version of the English national dish, Scotch roast sirloin of beef with Yorkshire pudding. And, if you like pork, you have to try their Gloucester old spot roast loin of pork with sage & onion stuffing & apple sauce. Finally, the home-made cottage pie with cheesy mashed potatoes and fresh veggies is... yummy.

If you're planning on dinner at the Plough, you'll need to make a reservation; lunch, just drop in and place your order.

Where to Stay:

The Plough is also a popular bed and breakfast inn, one I can highly recommend:

The Plough offers three guest rooms, each providing stunning views over the "glorious Cotswold countryside."

The guest rooms are situated in the Tallot, a quaint old stone stable building now converted into comfortable accommodations with all of the modern conveniences. The guest rooms include two family rooms with a double and single bed, and one double room, all with private bathrooms (showers) and all are beautifully decorated. And, of course, there is the lovely Cotswold garden for you and the kids to enjoy.

Rates:

Double or Twin £80.00 per night for two people

Single £60.00 per night (excluding Cheltenham Races and Bank Holidays)

Family of three sharing £100.00 per night

Family of four sharing £110.00 per night

All prices include Full English Breakfast.

This is a non-smoking establishment. No dogs.

Contact:

The Plough Inn at Ford, Temple Guiting, Cheltenham, Gloucestershire, GL54 5RU, England; Telephone 01386 584215 and 0800 066 3851

How to Get There:

Ford is on the B4077 about eight miles from Broadway, seven miles from Stow-on-the-Wold, 3 miles from Stanway and one mile from Temple Guiting.

The Slaughters

From Stow on the Wold, drive a couple of miles west along the Fosse Way (A429) to Copshill Road and turn right; from there it's less than a mile to Lower Slaughter; Upper Slaughter is less than a mile farther on.

Lever Slaughter – Courtesy of Margaret Sutton and Creative Commons

There's no doubt that these two picturesque little villages are two of the showpieces of the Cotswolds. The tiny river Eye that flows past the old corn mill is surely one of the most photographed spots in all England. Both Upper and Lower Slaughter are completely unspoiled, timeless, in fact. Visit the tiny tearooms for lunchtime snacks.

The Old Mill at Lower Slaughter – Courtesy of
Graham Taylor and Creative Commons

The Old Mill is at the western end of the village, built in the nineteenth century, it was last used commercially in 1958. The Mill now houses a small tea room and gift shop.

The name of the two villages is a little misleading. Slaughter, in this case, does not mean killing. The word Slaughter "stems from the Old English name for a wet land 'slough' or 'slothre' and literal translation might be "muddy place" which these two tiny villages are definitely not, at least not whenever I've visited.

Upper Slaughter – Copyright © Blair Howard

There once was a time when a visitor could wander the two villages and see very few other people. Not so today, as close as these two Cotswold villages are to Winchcome, Stow on the Wold and Bourton on the Water, they have today become tourist hotspots.

The Old Well at Lower Slaughter – Courtesy of Graham Horn and Creative Commons

The two villages are located along the banks of the River Eye, a narrow, shallow waterway that meanders through the center of both Lower and Upper Slaughter; add the traditional stone cottages, a three or four stone footbridges across the Eye, the Old Water Mill, and you have the makings of one of the most photogenic spots in the Cotswolds.

Upper Slaughter – Courtesy of Christine Matthews &
Creative Commons

Upper Slaughter is less than a mile away from Lower Slaughter; the two connected by the wandering River Eye.

The Slaughters have their roots set deep in Cotswold history, back even beyond Norman times when Upper Slaughter was dominated by a castle, of which only the motte and bailey (mound) remain.

Cottages in Upper Slaughter – Courtesy of Trevor
Rickard & Creative Commons

Upper Slaughter is famous not only for its chocolate box façade, but also for its beautiful gabled Manor House, one of the finest Elizabethan buildings in the area and now a hotel (see below).

The Manor House at Upper Slaughter – Courtesy of Natalia A McKenzie & Creative Commons,

Where to Stay:

The Lords of the Manor Hotel (see the photo above) is set in eight acres of landscaped gardens and rolling parkland. It's a place where you can relax and enjoy all the wonders of the Slaughters, and the surrounding market towns and attractions.

It's not inexpensive, but if you want to experience the best of the Cotswolds, this is as good a place as any to do it. The hotel is extremely well run, the staff friendly and helpful, the food excellent and, as always, you get what you pay for; but here, you may even get a little more.

Expect to pay between £199.00 and £495.00 for bed and breakfast. The rates are per room, per night and include a traditional breakfast and value added tax

For bed, breakfast and dinner expect to pay £320.00 and £625.00. These rates are per room, per night and include three course dinner from the A La Carte Menu in the Michelin starred Restaurant, a Full English breakfast and value added tax.

Contact: The Lords of the Manor, Upper Slaughter, Gloucestershire GL54 2JD; Telephone: 01451 820 243; Fax: 01451 820 696; reservations@lordsofthemanor.com

Northleach is just 9 miles west of Stow on the Wold and less than 6 miles from Bourton on the Water. From Bourton, or Stow, take the Fosse Way (A429). From Burford, take the A40 and drive north to Northleach. From Cirencester, take the Fosse Way east and drive about 10 miles; From Cheltenham, it's a drive of less than 15 miles.

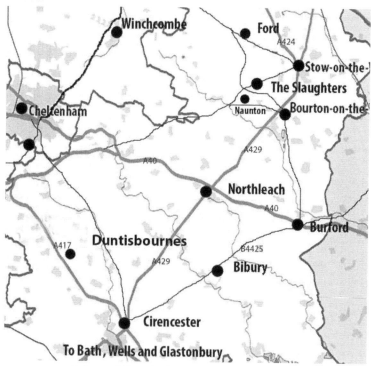

Map of South Central Cotswolds

So, as you can see, Northleach is central to the Cotswolds and thus it was central to its woolen industry.

Northleach Town Sign – Courtesy of Simon Atkin and Creative Commons

Small as Northleach is, the town has always been an important center for the Cotswolds. As long ago as the 800 it belonged to the Abbey of Gloucester, and in 1220 was granted its charter to hold a weekly market. But it was the wool trade that brought fame and fortune to the little market town. From 1340 to 1540 all things sheep related came to, or passed through, Northleach.

The High Street – Courtesy of Nick W and Creative Commons

During the Middle Ages, from the early 15th Century on, the wool industry in Northleach flourished and the town became extremely wealthy. And in fact, the tiny market town's most famous feature, its massive (by Cotswold standards) 15th century church of St Peter and St Paul is the product of that wool trade. The town today, reflects its wealthy past in its fine 15th Century through the 18th Century homes and commercial buildings.

Church of St Peter and St. Paul Northleach – Courtesy of Nick McNeill and Creative Commons

The church of St Peter and St Paul was built by the town's wool merchants. Stone for the church, was raised from the quarry in the town center, now the Market Square.

St. Peter and St. Paul is an amazing testament to the stonemason's art in the 15th Century. Within the church, you'll find many fine examples of memorial brasses – tombs with large, flat carved brass plates dedicated to the prominent members of the town's woolen industry that helped to pay for the church's construction and upkeep.

The Church Font – Courtesy of Hugh Llewelyn and
Creative Commons

The church of St. Peter and St. Paul is one of the finest,
and most beautiful, examples of the Perpendicular-style
church in the Cotswolds – Perpendicular being the
English Gothic name of the architectural style prevalent in
England from about 1180 until about 1520. The south
porch of the church with its pinnacles and niches
epitomizes Perpendicular architecture and is said be, "the
most lovely in all England."

The South Porch – Courtesy of Hugh Llewelyn and
Creative Commons

But the church's most glorious feature has to be its
great east window. Oh what a spectacle it makes when the
light floods in through the window.

The Great East Window – Courtesy of Hugh Llewelyn
and Creative Commons

So, Northleach is perhaps the ideal stop along either of
the two roads upon which it stands, either from Oxford to
Cheltenham, or between Stow and Cirencester. Its town
center has changed little over the past 600 years. Take a
little time to walk the narrow streets and alleys leading off
the marketplace and you'll discover old-world houses
with upper levels of timber framing.

Northleach is a great place to spend an afternoon.
There's something here for just about everyone, including
Post Office. Wine Bar, General Store, Chemist,
hairdressers, and superb butcher with a tempting deli
counter in the second

square, Mechanical Music Museum and Dolls House Collection.

The Old Prison is now home to a bistro type cafe, the Cotswold Lion Cafe, open every day serving light lunches and refreshment. The Old Prison is also home to the Escape to the Cotswolds visitor center, and the Rural Life Collection.

Best Pubs:

The Wheatsheaf Inn – Courtesy of Hugh Llewelyn and Creative Commons

The town has three pubs worth noting: The Sherborne Arms, The Red Lion Inn, and The Wheatsheaf Inn; speaking of which, The Wheatsheaf is one of the area's finest pubs, and a real favorite for locals and visitors.

Where to Stay:

Blanche House in Turkdean is an old-world family home set in the heart of the Cotswolds and centrally-located to Cirencester, Bourton-on-the-Water, Stow-on-the-Wold, Burford and Cheltenham. Blanche House is set on 500 picturesque acres of family farmland; The home is surrounded by pastoral meadows, woodland and ponds; it is in fact in an Area of Outstanding Natural Beauty.

"There are mown grass rides through the woods and out onto the fields, which guests are encouraged to explore. Inside, there are two bedrooms to choose from, as well as a drawing room with an open fireplace to relax in. A full English breakfast - and more - is served in the glass barn overlooking the gardens."

Expect to pay around £80 per night for bed and breakfast.

Blanche House, Turkdean, Gloucestershire GL54 3NX; 01451 861176; email@blanchehouse.com

Yew Tree Cottage Bed and Breakfast

This is what I'm talking about. When I'm looking for the quintessential Cotswold Bed And Breakfast, this would be it. Yew Tree Cottage is a delightful Cotswolds stone cottage in a peaceful rural hamlet offering Bed & Breakfast accommodation in an unrivalled stretch of the English countryside. Your host, Vivien Burford, has turned her cottage into the quintessential Cotswolds bed and breakfast home "providing every modern comfort in a very traditional setting. A perfect 'cottage break'!"

Ms. Burford offers afternoon teas in the gardens in the summer and open fires in the winter. Yew Tree Cottage has recently been refurbished and "provides new age comfort with old world charm."

The cottage is surrounded by beautifully landscaped gardens; the atmosphere is informal relaxed and the lady of the house specializes in "English home cooking with fresh home-baked breads and cakes and real local produce."

Accommodations at Yew Tree Cottage include two double guest rooms, one with an en-suite bathroom, the other has a private bathroom.

Contact: Vivien Burford, Yew Tree Cottage, Turkdean, CHELTENHAM, Gloucestershire, GL54 3NT; e-mail: vivien@bestcotswold.com, Phone: 01451 860 222

The Wheatsheaf Inn

The Wheatsheaf is an old-world coaching inn, now a popular public house (pub), modernized and transported into the 21st Century. The inn was a stop along the way between Cheltenham and London. Horses, drivers and passengers were housed overnight.

The Wheatsheaf Inn, Northleach – Courtesy Jonathan Billinger & Creative Commons

The old still looks much as it did in the 18th Century, but things have changed, for the better I think. The inn today features "14 beautiful bedrooms, a great wine list, good beer and some excellent regional food which is, wherever possible, local, seasonal and sourced from only the best suppliers in the area."

I have not stayed at the Wheatsheaf, but I have spent an evening – several in fact – in the bar and I know the pub quite well.

Contact: Wheatsheaf Inn, West End | Cotswolds, Northleach GL54 3EZ, England; Phone 01451 860244; Email reservations@cotswoldswheatsheaf.com

The village of Chedworth itself is a little off the beaten path, and not usually a stop on most tours, guided or otherwise… with one exception: its historic Roman Villa.

The Village of Chedworth – Courtesy Andy Chapple & Creative Commons

The village is some seven miles from Cirencester, five miles from Northleach and 11 miles from Cheltenham, close enough to the Fosse Way (the A429) to warrant a quick visit.

Chedworth is a pretty little Cotswold village, with its old-world, and not-so-old - Cotswold stone houses hugging the steep sides of the Coln River Valley. Unlike many of the villages in the Cotswolds, Chedworth remains unspoiled. A thriving little community, is just big enough to have its own village school, church, and pub.

The Seven Tuns Pub at the bottom of the lane –
Courtesy of Graham Horn & Creative Commons

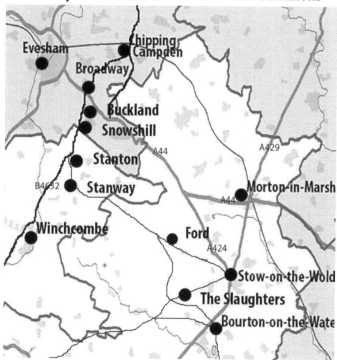

Map of South Central Cotswolds

Things to See:

Chedworth Roman Villa

As Cotswold historic sites go, the Roman Villa is probably one of the most popular. Dating back some 1,600 years, the Villa was home to some of the richest people in the country, that is until the fall of the Roman Empire when its legions were recalled to Rome and protectorates abandoned at the end of the 4th Century.

There's no doubt that Chedworth once was home to a high-ranking Roman official. The ruins indicate an extensive and luxurious complex complete with hypocaust (the central heating system of the day), baths and mosaic floors, all of which are on view to the public.

The Museum at Chedworth Roman Villa – Courtesy of Pam Brophy and Creative Commons

The complex represents one of the largest Romano-British villas in the country.

In the photo above you see a section of the mosaic floors at Chedworth Roman Villa - courtesy of Rob Farrow and Creative Commons

In the photo above, you see more of the mosaic floor, but also a section of the exposed hypocaust system - courtesy of Rob Farrow and Creative Commons

The Ruins at Chedworth Roman Villa – Courtesy of Shaun Ferguson & Creative Commons

The ruins have narrow paths for visitors to follow and view "some of the amazing inventions brought to this country by the Romans - including mosaics, bathhouses, latrines and hypocaust system. You can get close enough to the mosaics for photographs, and you can visit the museum to view an amazing collection of Roman tools, implements and artefacts discovered over the many years of excavations at the site.

The Nymphaeum. Seen in the photo above, was a water shrine. As was usual, this little pool is fed by a natural spring. The entire villa complex depended on a fresh supply of water, so it's not surprising that they wanted to keep the Water Spirits (or Nymphs) happy! Photo and description of the Nymphaeum are courtesy of Rob Farrow and Creative Commons.

Entrance fees: Adult: £8.80; Child: £4.40; Family: £22.00; Group adult: £7.95; Group child: £3.60

Contact: Chedworth Roman Villa is part of the national Trust. National Trust at Chedworth Roman Villa, Yanworth, near Cheltenham, GL54 3LJ; **Phone:** 01242 890256; **Email:** chedworth@nationaltrust.org.uk

Burford is another of those historic, little market towns for which the Cotswolds are so famous. And small it is. With a population of just over 1,000, it's a sleepy town that owes it wealth and fame to the wool trade. Located just 20 miles west of Oxford on the A40, and less that 10 miles from Stow on the Wold, Bourton on the Water and Northleach, Burford is your southern gateway into the Cotswolds.

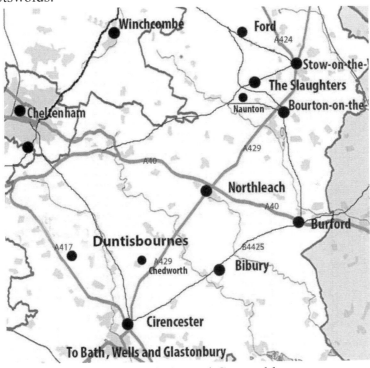

Map of South Central Cotswolds

It doesn't get much nicer than this. The scene in the photo above is of Burford High Street on a sunny afternoon in winter – Courtesy of John Shortland and Creative Commons.

No one is quite sure when the area was first settled, but it seems likely that people have inhabited what is now Burford since Neolithic times. The Domesday Book, 1086, William the Conqueror's tally of his new possessions in England records a small village of approximately 200. It was granted a charter to hold markets either in the late 11th or early 12th Centuries, exactly when, no one seems to know.

Today, Burford is a popular stop along the way into the Cotswolds. A busy, though unspoiled little community, its businesses have a "long tradition of good service and the supply of excellent luxury and essential goods to both residents and visitors." And so say we all.

Sheep Street, Burford – Courtesy of Martin Bodman & Creative Commons

Burford's High Street, not so very different from its Costwold peers, is lined with the old houses and cottages so typical of the area – all built from the same honey-colored stone. Burford is timeless; a microcosm of narrow side streets and alleyways separating the 17th and 18th Century buildings. Tiny shops, tearooms, art galleries and antiques shops offer a wealth of treasures and opportunities to enjoy that oh-so-typical English afternoon tea and cakes.

You'll also want to visit the splendid parish church, more cathedral than church, a product of the wealth that came to Burford during the era of the Cotswold wool trade

One of Burford's Alleyways – Courtesy Andy F &
Creative Commons

St John the Baptist Church, in Burford,

Wealth from wool gave the parish church of Saint John
the Baptist its current grandeur. The building was
completed in the late 1400s and its windows filled with
stained glass, of which only fragments remain. The
widows you see today are restorations carried out during
the early part of the 20th Century.

Church of John the Baptist, Burford – Courtesy of
Colin Smith & Creative Commons

The Whall Window in the Church of John the Baptist –
Courtesy of David Stowell & Creative Commons

Finally, you'll want to stroll the banks of the tiny River Windrush that meanders through the town; the same River Windrush you'll visit at Bourton on the Water.

The River Windrush at Burford – Courtesy of David Stowell & Creative Commons

Yes, Burford is, indeed, a beautiful little town. A fact that's not in dispute as Burford has been designated an Area of Outstanding Natural Beauty and is protected by the Cotswolds Conservation Board.

Burford is perfectly placed as base to explore the other famous towns and villages of the surrounding area including Oxford and Cheltenham and other attractions too.

Best Pubs:

The Mermaid Inn, Burford – Courtesy of Colin Smith & Creative Commons

The Lamb Inn, Burford – Courtesy of Peter Watkins & Creative Commons

Where to Stay:

The Lamb Inn

The Lamb Inn (see photo above) is one of those old-world English pubs now hotel. When I say old-world, I mean flag-stone floors, log fires, cozy sitting room and bar, four-poster beds and, of course, real ale. Expect to pay from £89 per night. Oh, and yes, the pub also has a great restaurant.

Contact: The Lamb Inn & Restaurant, Sheep Street, Burford Oxford Oxfordshire OX18 4LR; Phone 01993 823155. Email: info@lambinn-burford.co.uk

The Burford Hotel

The Burford Hotel on the High Street in Burford has seven guest rooms all with nice views, either of the High Street or the courtyard garden, two intimate sitting rooms - one with a log fire and honor bar and the other overlooking the courtyard. All guest rooms have complimentary mineral water, English toiletries, hair dryers, TV's and a collection of books and magazines. Burford House is open for breakfast, lunch and afternoon tea. Children are welcome.

Contact: Burford House, 99 High Street, Burford, Oxfordshire, OX18

The Cotswold Gateway Hotel

The Cotswold Gateway Hotel has 20 guest rooms, all with en-suite bathrooms, radio/alarm clock, TV, hairdryer, trouser press, telephone and welcome tray with tea/coffee.

Contact: The Cotswold Gateway Hotel 216, The Hill, Burford, Oxfordshire, OX18 4HX; Phone 01993 822695; Email: cotswldgateway@btconnect.com

Bibury

Bibury is a tiny Cotswold village known for its honey-colored seventeenth century stone cottages with steeply pitched roofs. William Morris, the father of the English Craft Movement in the late 19th century, called Bibury "the most beautiful village in England." And so it might be. For sure, it's one of the brightest jewels in the Cotswolds.

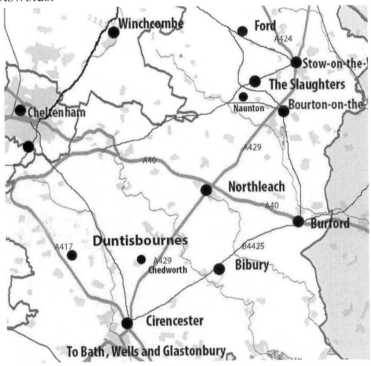

Map of South Central Cotswolds

I have lost count of the number of times I have walked the footpaths, trails and lanes of Bibury. I love this place. I love the peace and quiet, the stunningly beautiful views, the wildlife and, most of all, I love the overall feeling that this, the village of Bibury, really is what the English Cotswolds are all about.

The Swan Hotel on the River Coln at Bibury – Photo
Courtesy of Creative Commons and Saffron Blaze

The Arlington Row cottages were once the homes of
weavers who worked the cloth from the nearby Arlington
Mill. The place where the wool was hung to dry after
being washed in Arlington Row, was known as "Rack
Isle". Today, this water meadow and marshy area, which
is seasonally flooded and surrounded by water from three
sides, is an important habitat for water-loving plants and
birds including Mallards, Coots, and Moorhens; it is also
a National Trust Wildfowl Reserve with a footpath
running through it; it really is a lovely walk.

Bibury is old, one of the oldest settlements in the
Cotswolds. Mentioned in William the Conqueror's
Domesday Book of 1086, the survey records details of the
village then known as Becheberie, and that the lands and
church therein were held by St. Mary's Priory at
Worcester. Ownership of the village passed on to the
Abbey of Osney, near Oxford in 1130, and the Abbey
continued to hold it until the dissolution of the abbey in
1540.

Rack Isle Footpath – Photo Courtesy of Creative
Commons and Kenneth Allen

Bibury is a tiny, old-world collection of architecturally
significant Cotswold buildings and homes, the largest of
which is Bibury Court. Built in 1633, Bibury Court is a
Jacobean, Grade I listed building, and the one-time home
of Lord Sherborne. Today, Bibury Court is a hotel – more
about that later.

Church of Saint Mary – Photo Courtesy of Creative Commons and Philip Halling

The tiny Church of Saint Mary (above) is a Saxon structure and was, until the dissolution in 1540, part of Osney Abbey.

Arlington Row (see the photo below) is a stunningly beautiful row of honey-colored cottages that date from 1380. The cottages were once a monastic wool store but were converted into homes for local weavers in the 17th century. Today, Arlington Row is a popular visitor attraction, and one of the most photographed scenes in the Cotswold.

A note of trivia: American industrialist Henry Ford tried buy the entire Arlington Row. The idea being to ship it, stone-by-stone, back to Michigan so that he could incorporate it into Greenfield Village. The village was also the backdrop for the movies, Stardust and Bridget Jones's Diary.

Arlington Row, Bibury - Photo Courtesy of Creative Commons and Saffron Blaze

How to Get There:

Bibury is midway between Burford and Cirencester, South of the B4425 road.

Where to Stay:

There are just a couple of place to stay in Bibury Village; Bibury Court is one of them.

Bibury Court Hotel – Photo Courtesy of Creative Commons and Steve Daniels

Bibury Court is a historic, though relatively small, English country house in the village of Bibury. Now a somewhat upscale country hotel, surrounded by the stunning Cotswold countryside, it's a place where you can get a real feel for what it must have been like to live the privileged English country life of a century ago.

Today, Bibury Court provides a peaceful respite from the rigors of city life: relaxation and time... yes, just to smell the flowers. It really is a terrific place to stay, even if only for a single night.

Facilities at Bibury Court include 18 bedrooms, a very nice bar, a drawing room, and beautifully landscaped gardens. The property is bordered by the River Coln, close to the village, with footpaths and trails to explore.

Rates

"Double" Rooms - from £145

"Classic" Rooms - from £175

"Big Double" Rooms - from £235

"Grand" Rooms - from £255

The "Junior Suite" - from £295

The "Suite" - at £345

Prices are per night, and include a Continental Breakfast and VAT.

Contact:

Bibury Court Hotel, Bibury, Cirencester, Gloucestershire, GL7 5NT, England; Telephone 01285 740337; Email hello@biburycourt.com

The Swan Hotel, Bibury

The Swan Hotel is a charming 17th century former coaching inn set on the banks of the tiny River Coln in the village of Bibury. It's an old-world, peaceful setting perfect for a romantic break, or even as a jumping-off point for your visit to the Cotswolds.

The Swan Hotel at Bibury – Photo Courtesy of Creative Commons and David Stowell.

The atmosphere is friendly, the rooms are comfortable yet elegant, and the in-house restaurant serves great food and fine wine. The guestrooms all have private bathrooms and offer the best in Cotswold bed and breakfast.

Rates:

Standard Double/Twin Room £170 (midweek) or £210 (Friday/Saturday)

Superior Double/Twin Room £190 (midweek) or £230 (Friday/Saturday)

Superior Four Poster Room £230 (midweek) or £270 (Friday/Saturday)

Family Room £260 (midweek) or £340 (Friday/Saturday)

Garden Suite £290 (midweek) or £330 (Friday/Saturday)

Contact:

Swan Hotel, Bibury, Gloucestershire GL7 5NW, England; Telephone 01285 740695; Email info@swanhotel.co.uk

The Old House B&B at Calmsden

The Old House is a charming Bed and Breakfast set in the rural hamlet of Calmsden, less than 6 miles from Bibury. It's not a big place, far from it, but it does offer a warm and relaxed atmosphere, three comfortable guestrooms with private bathrooms, coffee/tea makers and flat screen TVs.

Breakfast is included in the rate and is served in the oak paneled dining room and includes home-made organic bread, jams, marmalade and fresh fruit.

Rates:

Doubles from £75.00

Double/Twin from £80.00 to £85.00

Single Room from £60.00

Contact:

Bridget Baxter, The Old House, Calmsden, Cirencester, Gloucestershire GL7 5ET, England;

Telephone 01285 831240; Email baxter@theoldhouse-calmsden.co.uk

Where to Eat:

There are two nice places to eat in Bibury, both of them are mentioned above:

The Swan Hotel Brasserie:

Breakfast, lunch and dinner is served daily from Monday to Saturday, luch is served on Sunday. Expect to pay £35.00 for a 3 Course meal; be prepared to dress smartly - no jeans or trainers/tennis shoes, this is a non-smoking facility. You should call ahead and book as reservation: Telephone 01285 740695

The Bibury Court

The restaurant at Bibury Court serves breakfast, lunch, afternoon teas, bar snacks and dinner every day of the week. Management lets us know that "Lunch and dinner can be as relaxed or as formal as you like." And that "Non-resident visitors are welcome for lunch, dinner, and Sunday afternoon tea," but you must make a reservation. Call 01285 740337

Cirencester is to some, but not to me, the "Capital of the Cotswolds." Maybe it once was, but I have always found it to be a little off the main Cotswold track. But again, that's just me. The fact is, Cirencester, from its earliest times, WAS a very important market. In Roman times, Cirencester - Corinium Dobunnorum - was the second largest town in Britain.

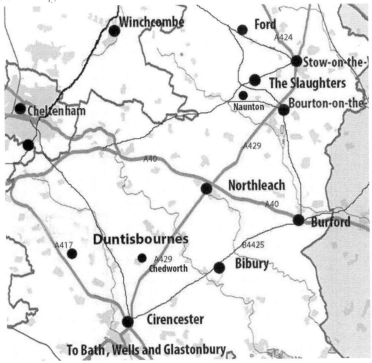

Map of South Central Cotswolds

Today, Cirencester is a quiet backwater with a serious history background. Although little remains of the bustling Roman city - just the imprint of the amphitheater - the town contains many interesting buildings, some dating back to medieval times.

Cirencester with the Roman Amphitheater at the right foreground – Courtesy of Richard Bird and Creative Commons

The market square is dominated by the town's Parish Church of St. John Baptist; more cathedral than church, it is one of the largest in England. Its south porch with its incredible fan vaulting was built about 1490. The church itself was founded in 1117 by King Henry 1. Back then, it was not the impressive structure it is today. Over the years it has been expanded, wings and porches have been added, most of it paid for by wealthy Cotswold wool merchants.

The Market Place with the Church of St. John the Baptist in the background - – Courtesy of Steve Daniels and Creative Commons

Perhaps, no, for sure, the church's most impressive features are its fan vaulting and stained glass windows. Another interesting feature is the church's beautiful pulpit, one of very few in the country to survive the Reformation.

Photo Courtesy of Steve Daniels and Creative Commons

Cirencester has been a market town since the early Norman period, as is mentioned in the Doomsday Book of 1086. Today the tradition is still observed: market traders set up their stalls every Monday and Friday selling all sorts of arts, crafts, antiques, fruit and vegetables and even antiques. That being so, Monday and Friday are the best days to visit.

The River Churn at Cirencester- – Courtesy of Brian
Robert Marshall and Creative Commons

Oh, and do not forget to visit Cirencester Park. It's a
great place to spend a couple of quiet hours with the
family and there are one or two interesting sights to see as
well, including the Round House you see in the photo
below.

The Round House in Cirencester Park – Courtesy of
Mike Baldwin and Creative Commons

Bibury Court Hotel

You might like to try this beautiful 18-bedroom country house hotel set in six acres of gardens and on the banks of the River Coln. The hotel is just outside of Cirencester on the edge of the village of Bibury, described by William Morris as "the most beautiful village in England."

Bibury Court is an ideal base for a tour of this western section of the Cotswolds: it's situated within an hour's drive of Oxford, Bath and Stratford upon Avon.

Rates: Expect to pay between £145 and £345 per night, depending upon the room.

Contact: Bibury Court Hotel, Bibury, Cirencester, Gloucestershire, GL7 5NT; Phone 01285 740337; Fax: 01285 740660; Email: hello@biburycourt.com

Riverside House

The Riverside House offers B&B accommodations at very reasonable rates. Facilities include 24 guest rooms, all with en-suite bathrooms, TV, direct dial telephone, trouser press and tea, coffee making facilities and Internet access available by prior arrangement.

The hotel is just a 15 minute walk from Cirencester's town center and is within easy reach of Stow, Cheltenham, Winchcombe, Bath, Northleach, the Slaughters and Burford.

Rates: expect to pay from £55.50 for a single room and from £71.00 for a double, per night. Group discounts are available.

Contact: Riverside House, Watermoor, Cirencester, Gloucestershire, GL7 1LF: Phone 1285 647642; Fax: 1285 647615; email: riversidehouse@mitsubishi-cars.co.uk

There are several of them, including Duntisbourne Leer, Duntisbourne Abbots, Duntisbourne Rouse and Middle Duntisbourne. All of them are within easy walking distance of one another. The Duntisbournes are located in the Gloucestershire, within the Cotswolds, less than five miles from Cirencester, 15 miles from Northleach, and 11 miles from Cheltenham.

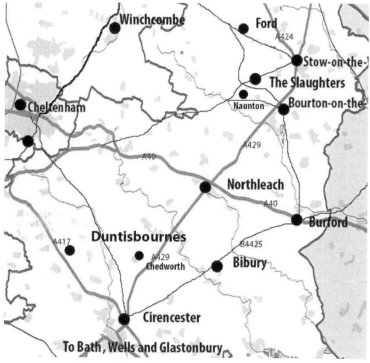

Map of South Central Cotswolds

There are a number of reasons why you should go out of your way to visit this collection of tiny villages: they are visually stunning, as are almost all Cotswold villages; there are several important sites to visit, not the least of which is St. Michael's Church in Duntisbourne Rouse;

and the Five Mile House in Duntisbourne Abbots is famous for its fine pub food across the Cotswolds.

The Ford at Duntisbourne Rouse - Photo Courtesy of Creative Commons and Saffron Blaze

The original village predates the Norman Conquest. It was, in fact, was recorded as Duntesborne, a slightly different spelling, in King William's Domesday Book of 1086.

The Ford at Duntisbourne Leer - Photo Courtesy of Creative Commons and Saffron Blaze

Duntisbourne Abbots is where you'll find the Five Mile House, which has been a pub for more than 300 years; oh what stories those old walls could tell. Duntisbourne Abbots is also where you'll find Peter's Church. Built in the 12th century, on the site of an earlier Saxon church, the tower is Norman and has "belfry lights of pierced stone lattice work that date from the 13th century." The font also dates from Norman times, while the chancel arch is much later and dates from the Victorian era.

Duntisbourne Rouse boasts of another, much older church. St Michael's Church Anglican church was built is Saxon times, before the Norman Conquest, but the chancel was added in Norman times, as were the windows. St. Michael's is a Grade I listed building.

The church is constructed of limestone, probably gathered in the fields around the village, with hand-hewn stone tiles on the roof.

St. Peter's Church at Duntisbourne Rouse - Photo Courtesy of Creative Commons and Saffron Blaze

The Crypt in St. Peter's Church Duntisbourne Rouse -
Photo Courtesy of Creative Commons and Norman Hyett

Of great interest, and a must-see for visitors, is the small, Norman barrel-vaulted crypt located under the chancel (above). The crypt dates to the early 11th century and is reached via a flight of narrow stone steps. What the crypt might have been used for, no one knows.

Where to Eat:

Five Mile House

Five Mile House, beside the A417 at Duntisbourne Abbots, is known far and wide for its fine "pub grub." The House serves traditional English food - home-made pies, fresh fish, steaks and grills – for lunch and evening meals daily. The House also offers the best range of real ales that you're likely to find anywhere in the Cotswolds. I can personally recommend the grilled salmon and, of course, the inevitable Ploughman's Lunch.

Contact: The Five Mile House, Duntisbourne Abbots, Cirencester, Gloucestershire, GL7 7JR; Telephone 01285 821432; Email fivemile@btconnect.com

Well, they do say that Castle Combe is 'The Prettiest Village in England,' and it's hard to argue with the sentiment, really. You only have to look at the photographs to understand why. But all that's pretty does not always make for a happy populace. First, it's a really tiny village; second, it can be very busy, especially during the tourist season. And pretty is what has attracted numerous film makers over the years, causing disruption to the oh-so-idyllic way of life in and around the village. Even so, you will find the villagers welcoming and friendly and, close as castle Combe is to Bath, it would be a shame not to visit this stunningly beautiful Cotswold village.

Castle Combe - Photo Courtesy of Creative Commons and Saffron Blaze

The center piece of the village is its 14th century market cross, but Castle Combe's history dates back much further than that, well into the dark ages, in fact. The hill overlooking the village was fortified in Neolithic times, and then by the Romans, Anglo Saxons and finally the Normans. Today, nothing but some ancient earthworks remain.

Water Street - Castle Combe - Photo Courtesy of Creative Commons and John Menard

During the Middle Ages, Castle Combe was an important center for the burgeoning Cotswold wool industry and the local artisans lived in the cottages. Today, the village is one of the most visited spots in the Cotswolds, and has been used extensively by the movie industry, playing host to film crews from around the world: Doctor Doolittle was filmed in and around Castle Combe, as was the War Horse, and one of those inevitable Agatha Christie epics, The Murder of Roger Ackroyd. one of the Poirot episodes, The Wolfman, etc.

Many of the village homes are listed buildings, some are hundreds of years old, all are constructed from that same honey colored limestone found all across these hills and dales. Even the roofs are covered with stone slates/tiles made from split limestone.

How to Get There:

Castle Combe is approximately 12 miles from the city of Bath. Take the A4 London Road to its junction with

Bannerdown Road; take Bannerdown Road to the A420 and turn right then left to Castle Combe.

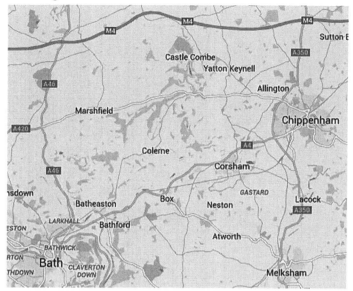

Map Courtesy of Google Maps

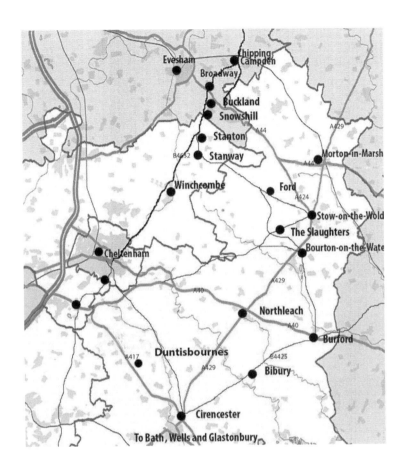

The City of Bath was first established by the Romans sound the 60Ad and was given the Latin name of Aquae Sulis which, roughly translated, means "the waters of Sulis" Sulis is the shortened form of the name of the Romano-British goddess Sulis Minerva, a deity worshiped at the thermal spring; lead tablets found at the baths suggest that she was an important mother goddess both to the Romans and to local Celtic population.

The geothermally-heated waters of the spring were said to have healing powers, thus the Romans built baths and a temple on the surrounding hills and around hot springs and Bath became an important center for the Roman Empire in Britain, and it continued as such until its legions were recalled to Rome at the end of the 4th century. The great bath house built by the Romans is one of the city's most important historic sites.

The City of Bath – Courtesy of Derek Harper and Creative Commons

In the photo above you have an overview of the City of Bath as seen from Beechen Cliff: Bath Abbey and north-eastern Bath dominates this view of the city. Curving crescents form the other dominant feature, with Camden

Crescent at upper left, The Paragon below it, Camden Road is above the abbey, and Belgrave Crescent is just below that.

The Roman Baths – Courtesy Steve Cadman and Creative Commons

Bath has been a place of Christian worship on this site for more than 1,000. The Anglo-Saxon Abbey built in mid-700 was demolished by the Norman conquerors of England in 1066 and construction of new one began around 1090. Unfortunately it fell victim to King Henry VIII and the Dissolution of the monasteries in the late 1539 century.

The Abbey Church at Bath – Copyright © Blair
Howard

The present Abbey Church, impressive as it is, is quite
young compared to many of its peers around the country;
Construction began in 1499 but was not completed until
1611. Over the preceding centuries, going back into the
dark ages, the churches that stood on this spot have
witnessed an astounding tapestry of the area's history.

The City of Bath was awarded World Heritage Site
status in 1987, and rightly so. There is so much to see and
do in Bath, not the least of which is the great Roman Bath
House and the city's incredible architecture.

The Royal Crescent at Bath – Copyright © Blair Howard

More than 4 million people visit the city each year, and I warrant that few leave disappointed.

Where to Stay:

Brooks Guesthouse

Guesthouse is really just another word for Bed and Breakfast, although many do offer an evening meal. Brooks guesthouse offers bed and breakfast accommodation in downtown Bath. The guesthouse has 21 bedroom, single and double, all with private bathrooms, "new pocket sprung mattresses, high quality cotton bed linen, fluffy bath sheets, flat screen TV's and DVD players, digital radios and I-pod docking stations." Sounds good to me.

Breakfast at Brooks is quite an experience: you'll have the choice of a full English breakfast, vegetarian breakfast, smoked salmon and scrambled eggs, homemade muesli or granola and organic yoghurt. Most of the ingredients are sourced locally. Access to the internet is available free in the guest lounge; Wi-Fi is available throughout the guesthouse.

Parking at Brooks will cost you a little extra: 24h Parking permits are available for £8, but are available only on a first come first served basis. Failing that, you can use the nearby Charlotte Street Car Park – just a short 5 minute walk away – but that will set you back £18.50 per 24 hours.

Rates: Expect to pay between £59.00 and £89.00 for a single room; £79.00 to £119.00 for a double; and between £120.00 to £170.00 for a family room. Rates are per night per room and breakfast is included.

Contact: Brooks Guesthouse, 1 Crescent Gardens, Upper Bristol Road, Bath, BA1 2NA' Phone 01225 425543; Fax: 01225 318147; Email: info@brooksguesthouse.com

Royal Park Guest House

Royal Park Guest house is also located at Crescent Gardens and is only a short 5 minute walk away from all of the sights and attractions of Bath; better yet, the guesthouse has its own private parking available free of charge for its guests. That alone is worth the cost of the room, which is quite reasonable. All of the rooms have a private bath (en-suite) along with TVs, hairdryer's, etc. High speed wireless internet access is available, too.

Rates: Expect to pay between £45.00 and £60.00 for a single room; £70.00 to £100.00 for a double room; and £150.00 to £140.00 for a family room. Rates are per room per nigh and breakfast is included.

Contact: Royal Park Guest House, 16 Crescent Gardens, Bath, BA1 2NA; Phone 01225 317651; Fax: +44 01225 423104; Email info@royalparkbath.co.uk.

Dolphin Cottage (Self Catering)

If you like to do it yourself, you might like to consider a self-catering stay in Bath. And there's probably nowhere better that Dolphin Cottage in Freshford, just five miles outside of Bath, to do it. Dolphin Cottage is a

17th century, Cotswold stone cottage, fully restored and overlooking the beautiful Cotswold countryside.

The cottage has three bedrooms, sleeping between one and five people, a modern luxury kitchen (fully equipped) and is comfortably furnished. Children of are welcome, but pets are not allowed. The cottage has its own private garden with a terrace, garden furniture and a barbeque. Best of all, the cottage has on-site parking. Freshford has both bus and train service into Bath, which means you can leave your car at the cottage and not have to worry about finding parking in the city.

Rates: Expect to pay a very reasonable £390 to £850 per week, including electricity, heating, hot water, bed linen and towels. The rates are dependent upon the season and the number of guests.

Contact: Dolphin Cottage, Freshford, Bath, BA2 7UQ; Phone 01225 722100; Email info@bath-holidaycottages.co.uk.

So, there you have it, my own version of the Cotswolds where I grew up. Is it a complete guide to the Cotswolds? No, far from it. It is, however, an overview of the most popular locals, and what you can expect to see, do and enjoy on your visit, along with some off-the-beaten path spots along the way that are dear to me. If I have missed your favorite spot, please send me an email and I'll be glad to include it in the next edition

Oh, and by the way, some folks have requested I include locations and attractions outside the Cotswold area. Where practical, I have done so, but some were requests for places far outside the Cotswold limits, including Warwick, Warwick Castle, Stratford-upon-Avon, and so on. These are all covered in detail in my other guide, the **Visitor's Guide to Shakespeare Country**. So, if you plan to visit Shakespeare Country while on your visit to the Cotswolds, you might want to grab a copy of that book too. You'll find the link on the next page.

I sincerely hope you enjoyed this book. Thank you so much for downloading it.

If you have comments of questions, you can contact me by email. I will reply to all emails. And you can also visit my website to view my blog, and for a complete list of my books.

If you enjoyed the book, I would really appreciate it if you could take a few moments and share your thoughts by posting a review on Amazon.

Visitor's Guide to Shakespeare Country
http://www.amazon.com/dp/B00IPKWRBC

Visitor's Guide to London
http://www.amazon.com/dp/B00HZ1FXL8